Introduction

The classic stories of childhood are a rich part of the world's literary heritage. Tales such as *Little Red Riding Hood*, *Cinderella*, *The Sleeping Beauty* and *Snow White* have universal appeal not only because they are imbued with a magic that allows the reader to get lost in a world of make-believe, but also because they deal with the complexities of human relationships, love and friendship, and the triumph of good over evil.

Storytelling is an ancient and intrinsic part of culture and language, and folk tales have been passed down from generation to generation in both the oral and written traditions, often going through innumerable changes along the way. Indeed, many different countries have their own variations of essentially the same tales. This process is still going on today, as authors and illustrators continue to create inspired and fresh adaptations of folk and fairy tales. This guide hopes to provide a glimpse of the wonderful array of books that are currently available.

This book came about as a result of a collaboration between Booktrust and the Children's Bookshow, which starts during National Children's Book Week (held in the first full week of October every year). We saw an opportunity to expand upon the theme of the 2004 Children's Bookshow – Folk and Fairy Tales – with an introductory guide that celebrates this wonderful field of children's literature.

As we compiled the guide, we encountered some problems of terminology. 'Folk tale' and 'fairy tale' are often used as interchangeable terms, which made it difficult

Introduction

to categorise some of the books under review. As Kevin Crossley-Holland explains in his foreword, 'folk-tale is a generic name' that encompasses many types of tale, including fairy tales and legends. 'Traditional tale' is the most appropriate term that covers all types of tale; however, to be consistent with the Children's Bookshow, we have used their title, Folk and Fairy Tales, for our Guide.

We have tried to bring together, in one unique volume, a selection of folk tales, fairy tales, myths, legends and modern versions of fairy tales. Stories by Charles Perrault, the Brothers Grimm and Hans Christian Andersen are complemented by lesser-known folk tales from around the world. It has been impossible to include everything, but we hope we have provided a broad cross-section of titles that will appeal to everyone.

How to use the Guide

The Guide has been divided into three broad sections: 'Folk and Fairy Tales' (which also includes fables and traditional tales from around the world); 'Myths and Legends'; and 'Modern Versions of Fairy Tales'. Each section, where possible, has been divided into four age categories (under 6; 6-8; 8-11; and 11+), which are intended to act only as a broad guideline; in fact, many of the books will appeal to a wide age-range, including adults.

The Guide also includes: a short article about Hans Christian Andersen (2005 marks the bicentenary of his birth); a bibliography of secondary sources; and an index of authors and titles. At the time of going to press, all the books in the guide were in print.

We hope that you will have as much fun using this Guide as we have had compiling it.

Deborah Hallford and Edgardo Zaghini
Editors

Foreword

Kevin Crossley-Holland taught for some years at a university in the American Midwest, and now lives in North Norfolk. In addition to writing for children, Kevin writes poetry for adults, translates from Anglo-Saxon and has collaborated with composers on two operas (including the children's opera The Green Children, composed by Nicola LeFanu), music-theatre and songs. He is a true disciple of North-West European culture, past and present, and many of his bestselling titles are featured in this publication.

One of the wonderful things about fairy tales, legends, myths, traditional tales of all kinds, is that most of them belonged to our grandparents' grandparents and most will belong to our grandchildren's grandchildren.

Like King Arthur, alive and asleep under a hill, always returning, they link generations. They were, and are, and will be.

Another wonder is the way in which a traditional tale must constantly change in order to survive, and yet always remains essentially the same.

And a third wonder, well, I'll come to that!

Let me quickly try to define the different kinds of traditional tale.

A **myth** is part of a jigsaw of tales, chiefly about goddesses and gods but also human beings and the whole order of creation. These deities mirror the characteristics, activities and values of the culture that creates them, but have vigorous, idiosyncratic lives of their own. I find it useful to think of myths as explanations or revelations of the physical world, our social behaviour and spiritual longings.

Folk tale is a generic name, a kind of grab-bag containing brief tales of many kinds. These involve humans, animals and supernatural beings, and illustrate our day-to-day lives with all their hopes, fears, small challenges, frustrations, rewards, punishments, dangers and absurdities.

One kind of folk tale, **legend**, has at its heart historical actuality in the same way that each pearl contains a piece of grit. The stories about Robin Hood and Oliver Cromwell are legends, and so are the stories we tell ourselves about our own early childhood: such curious mixtures of memory and invention, fact and fiction.

In the **fairy tale**, humans and supernatural beings meet, and humans are often rewarded or pay the price of disrespect. And then there are tales of fabulous beasts and shape-changers, fables, nursery stories, wonder-tales, ghost stories, jocular tales and tales about giants, stories of saints and devils, urban legends. All of these are folk tales.

True, poets and novelists, visual artists and film-makers regularly use themes (known in the trade as motifs) drawn from traditional tale, but most direct retellings are now written and illustrated with children in mind. Short, vivid and seldom introspective, myths and folk-tales not only help a child to decode the mysterious, often threatening, world she or he is growing into, but have the power to quicken a child's imagination in an intense way that is rewarding in itself and sows the seeds of a lifelong passion for story.

In the classroom, meanwhile, teachers put traditional tale to work in any number of ways: to develop logical and predictive thought; for language work; as the basis for discussions about action and consequence, right and wrong, religious belief, the existence of magic; for history and geography projects; and for translation into drama and music, dance and artwork.

But when European folklorists began to collect stories in the early nineteenth century, they regarded folk-tales as being just that: the tales of the illiterate folk – a great hoard passed from mouth to mouth, to be enjoyed by everyone.

These folklorists, men like the Brothers Grimm in Germany and Asbjornsen in Norway, Grundtvig in Denmark and Arnason in Iceland, had to race against time: against the dislocation of rural communities as people got swept up in the Industrial Revolution, against the growth of literacy and proliferation of newspapers, against the soft option of mechanical entertainment. These things all militated against the social importance and survival of the folk-tale.

There is so much for storytellers, now enjoying such a lively revival in Britain, and writers to learn from early descriptions of storytellers in action: their authority and readiness not only to tell but comment, their vividness and accuracy of language, their constant changes of mood, their use of face and hands, and their sense of delight both in telling and sharing. I've made a list of these attributes and stuck them on a wall, and try to face up to them each day.

What is for sure is that there are more retellings of traditional tale available today than ever before. There is a riot of individual tales, collections, anthologies, adaptations and novels that use traditional patterns and themes. The purpose of this excellent Guide is to select and review some of these books.

I believe any writer or illustrator in this field has responsibilities. One is to inhabit rather than plunder the world of traditional tale and another is to familiarise oneself with the culture from which a chosen tale comes. Any writer or illustrator has to contemplate what a specific tale actually means, and only then start to search for the appropriate form, words and images.

The last responsibility is, of course, to the author's and illustrator's audience. What, for instance, about the casual violence and downright cruelty that are part and parcel of folktale? The offensive sexism and stereotyping? And the almost invariably rural setting when the majority of us live in towns and cities? How is one to address such issues with children in mind?

As this Guide makes apparent, the best of our authors and illustrators face up to these challenges triumphantly. Its publication is timely, for fifteen years have passed since Mary Steele compiled her outstanding Signal Bookguide, *Traditional Tales*, and each season brings many additions (and, alas, deletions) to the books in print.

And now, the third wonder...

The third wonder is the way in which traditional tales manage to have the best of both worlds. On one hand, they tell us we're all in many ways the same, because we're all human beings. On the other, they show us how different we are, each of us, because we're individuals, and children of different ethnic groups, religions, cultures and geographical areas.

Failure to allow for and understand these differences has so often led to intolerance, persecution and war. But in celebrating them while identifying all we have in common, traditional tales reach out and invite us to draw closer to one another.

Kevin Crossley-Holland
August 2004

Folk & Fairy Tales

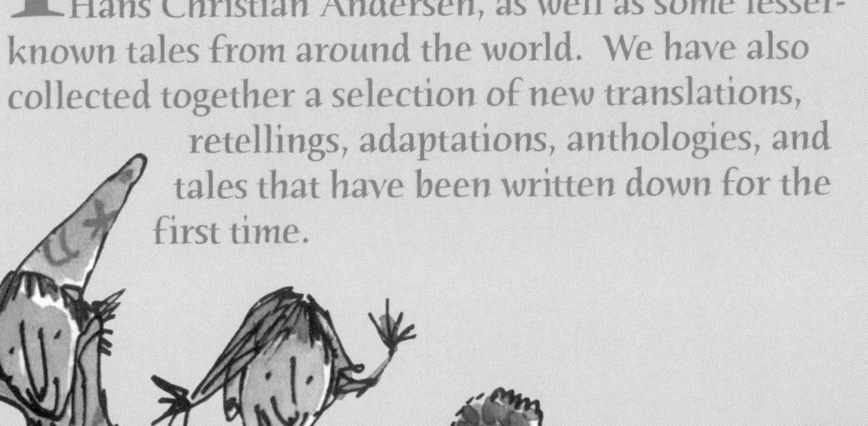

In this section you will find well-known fairy tales by Charles Perrault, the Brothers Grimm, and Hans Christian Andersen, as well as some lesser-known tales from around the world. We have also collected together a selection of new translations, retellings, adaptations, anthologies, and tales that have been written down for the first time.

Folk & Fairy Tales

The Ugly Duckling
Ian Beck

Orchard (1999) PB £4.99
ISBN: 1 84121 045 5

The Ugly Duckling
Kevin Crossley-Holland
illustrated by Meilo So

Orion (2001) HB £9.99
ISBN: 1 85881 838 9

The Ugly Duckling is one of Hans Christian Andersen's most poignant tales, the story of a long-necked duckling with grey and spiky plumage who is teased and rejected by his yellow, soft and fluffy siblings. Ian Beck's version, accompanied by his beautiful, warm and atmospheric illustrations, features an irresistibly appealing ugly duckling, and is an ideal picture book to read aloud. Kevin Crossley-Holland has used his skills as a renowned storyteller to bring a poetic magic to his adaptation, but he has kept closely to Andersen's original tale. Meilo So's fantastic watercolours enhance the story without overpowering it; her characterful animals are set against wonderful scenes of the changing seasons.

The Gingerbread Man
Hugh Lupton
illustrated by Diana Mayo

Barefoot (2003) PB £4.99
ISBN: 1 84148 930 1

This picture book lends itself perfectly to being read aloud and is ideal for introducing well-known nursery characters to young children. The Gingerbread Man, or Johnny Cake as his creators named him, is up to mischief from the moment he escapes from the oven to his final encounter with Mr Fox, who gobbles him up. Short sentences, colourful illustrations and plenty of repetition make this book ideal for children who are starting to read. The clear and bold type is very attractive, and the bright illustrations by Diana Mayo have been magnificently executed to accompany the text. An extra bonus, for all those who would like to put their culinary skills into practice, is the gingerbread recipe at the end of the book.

Don't Cry, Sly!
Henriette Barkow
illustrated by
Richard Johnson

Mantra (2002) PB £7.50
ISBN: 1 85269 663 X

Sly's mum is always bossing him around and the poor little fox is fed up with the way he is treated. Next door lives Little Red Hen, who becomes very nervous when Sly is sent to find a roast chicken for dinner. However, the quick-thinking hen comes up with a plan to suit them all. The pictures are wonderful, expressive and highly atmospheric. This dual language picture book is written in Tamil and English, and is available in 20 other language editions. A wonderful book to read aloud, it is ideal for children with English as a second language and would lend itself well to classroom use, particularly in multicultural schools.

Folk & Fairy Tales

The Emperor and the Nightingale
Meilo So

Frances Lincoln (1999) PB £4.99
ISBN: 0 7112 1416 6

The Emperor of China lives in a magnificent porcelain palace surrounded by the most beautiful objects in the world. However, the most beautiful thing of all – the song of the Nightingale – does not belong to him. The Nightingale agrees to sing for the Emperor, but is subsequently forced to live at the palace. When the Emperor is given a richly bejewelled mechanical bird, the real Nightingale is usurped and forgotten. Meilo So's striking retelling of one of the most popular Hans Christian Andersen tales is accompanied by her dazzling watercolours, which are full of nineteenth-century Chinese detail.

Goldilocks and the Three Bears
Valeri Gorbachev

North-South Books (2001) HB £9.99
ISBN: 0 7358 1438 4

This is an irresistible version of a nursery favourite. When a young girl walking in the woods discovers an empty house that belongs to a family of bears, she sets about making herself comfortable by eating their food and using their belongings. Valeri Gorbachev's humorous illustrations present a delightful family of bears and are filled with homely detail. Children will be entertained by the bemused reaction of the bears to their intruder. A great book for reading aloud.

The Gigantic Turnip
Aleksei Tolstoy
illustrated by Niamh Sharkey

Barefoot (1998) PB £5.99
ISBN: 1 902283 29 5

The Giant Turnip
Henriette Barkow
illustrated by
Richard Johnson

Mantra (2001) PB £7.50
ISBN: 1 85269 7881

Here are two different versions of an amusing Russian tale that was first recorded by Aleksei Tolstoy in the nineteenth-century. In *The Gigantic Turnip* an elderly couple, who live with their animals in a crooked cottage, grow vegetables in their large overgrown garden. However, they are in for a surprise when they grow a turnip so big that they cannot get it out of the ground! The illustrations by Niamh Sharkey of the couple, their army of animals and the turnip itself convey the humour of this folk tale, and young children will really enjoy following them as they try to remove the turnip from the ground. In *The Giant Turnip*, adapted by Henriette Barkow, the children in Miss Honeywood's class decide to grow vegetables in their school garden. What a shock they get when they discover a huge turnip that they are unable to move! This is a dual language picture book in Russian and English with colourful illustrations by Richard Johnson.

Folk & Fairy Tales

The Tortoise and the Hare: An Aesop's Fable

Angela McAllister
illustrated by Jonathan Heale

Frances Lincoln (2002) PB £5.99
ISBN: 0 7112 1805 6

This is one of Aesop's most well-known fables: the boastful conceit of a Hare pitted against the dogged determination and wisdom of a Tortoise. Although Aesop's fables were not composed originally for children, they have, over the years, been retold for younger audiences. This fable's distinct and important moral (that boastful conceit can be outwitted by wisdom) is expertly retold by Angela McAllister, and accompanied by amusing and perceptive woodcut illustrations by Jonathan Heale (winner of the Kurt Maschler Award in 1997).

The Famous Adventure of a Bird-Brained Hen

Jessica Souhami

Frances Lincoln (2004) PB £5.99
ISBN: 0 7112 2026 3

This adaptation of the well-known English folk tale *Henny Penny* tells the story of a hen who thinks that the sky is falling down when she is hit on the head by a falling acorn. On her way to tell the King, she relates her tale of woe to a duck, a chicken, a goose and a fox. There is plenty of humour and repetition in this popular story, which will keep young children entertained for hours. Writer and illustrator Jessica Souhami is also a puppeteer, whose travelling company uses colourful shadow puppets and music to accompany their storytelling. The influence of this theatricality is clearly evident in this lively and colourful book.

The Three Billy Goats Gruff

Mary Finch
illustrated by
Roberta Arenson

Barefoot (2001) PB £4.99
ISBN: 1 84148 350 8

The Three Billy Goats Gruff

Henriette Barkow
illustrated by
Richard Johnson

Mantra (2001) PB £7.50
ISBN: 1 85269 622 2

Here are two versions of a popular fairy tale. Three goats called Gruff (small, middle and large) live on the side of a steep hill and spend their days munching the green grass. Once their grass has been eaten up, they decide to cross to the other side of the bridge, where there is fresh green grass in abundance. Unfortunately, a horrible, hungry troll lives beneath the bridge and he is desperate to gobble them up! Mary Finch's humorous retelling of this story and the expressive collage-type illustrations by Roberta Arenson will appeal to children. The text is perfectly paced and punctuated to help adults read the story aloud. Henriette Barkow's edition of this tale also reads well, and Johnson's superb illustrations, particularly of the troll, are highly original. This edition is published as a dual language edition in Spanish and English.

Folk & Fairy Tales

Rainbow Bird: An Aboriginal Folk Tale from Northern Australia

Eric Maddern
illustrated by
Adrienne Kennaway

Frances Lincoln (1996) PB £5.99
ISBN: 0 7112 0898 0

This story is based on a fire myth of the Dalabon people of the Beswick Reserve in the Northern Territory of Australia. 'Long ago, in the Time of Dreams when the world was being born, there lived a rough, tough Crocodile Man. He was huge and mean and scary, and he had one thing nobody else had. Fire!' (And in Adrienne Kennaway's watercolours, he really is huge, mean and scary.) Crocodile Man won't share his precious gift with any of the other creatures, so, in despair, Bird Woman decides to steal it from him. The story, simply told, is brought to life by the rich colours in the illustrations, which evoke the barren beauty of the Australian landscape.

Mama God, Papa God: A Caribbean Tale

Richardo Keens-Douglas
illustrated by
Stefan Czernecki

Tradewind Books (2000) PB £4.95
ISBN: 1 896580 24 6

This creation tale from the Caribbean portrays Mama God and Papa God talking together as they add new elements to the heavens – the stars, the moon, the sun, and the earth. With love, laughter and delight, Papa God creates the first man and Mama God creates the first woman. On the earth they place trees and flowers, animals and birds, water and fish, wind and rain, and people of all shapes, colours and sizes. Finally they agree that the world they have made is a 'truly wonderful place'. The colourful, vibrant illustrations by Stefan Czernecki bring this well-known Caribbean tale alive.

Anancy and Mr Dry-Bone

Fiona French

Frances Lincoln (1992) PB £5.99
ISBN: 0 7112 0787 9

Clever Anansi and Boastful Bullfrog: A Caribbean Tale

'H' Patten
illustrated by
John Clementson

Frances Lincoln (2000) PB £5.99
ISBN: 0 7112 1401 8

As 'H' Patten explains in an afterword to his book, Anansi stories came originally from West Africa and subsequently travelled to the Caribbean with the slaves. Anansi is a magical character, sometimes represented as a spider, sometimes a man; sometimes he is good, and sometimes he is bad, as these two books demonstrate. In 'H' Patten's story, which is enlivened by John Clementson's colourful paper collage illustrations, Anansi spider's jealousy of Bullfrog gets the better of him, but Bredda Patoo the owl saves the day. Fiona French's story – a perennial picture book favourite – tells the story of Anancy the Man's efforts to woo Miss Louise in the face of competition from Mr Dry-Bone. The simple text and atmospheric illustrations bring this charming tale to life.

Under 6

Folk & Fairy Tales

Pirican Pic and Pirican Mor

Hugh Lupton
illustrated by Yumi Heo

Barefoot (2003) PB £5.99
ISBN: 1 84148 071 1

This is a retelling of a well-known Hebridean folk tale. It is about two friends, Pirican Pic and Pirican Mor, who decide to collect walnuts. Mor climbs up the walnut tree and throws the walnuts down to Pic, but Pic cracks them open and eats them all up. Mor wants to take revenge and asks the tree for a stick to 'whack and thwack Pic'. But the tree directs him to an axe, the axe to a stone, the stone to water and so on. As the story unfolds, the sentences get longer so that children can join in and learn or repeat them. This is an ideal story for reading aloud and for storytime sessions. The illustrations are colourful, cheerful and full of expression and there is a different typeface for each sentence to represent the various parts of the story.

Jack and the Beanstalk

Richard Walker
illustrated by Niamh Sharkey

Barefoot (2002) PB £4.99
ISBN: 1 901223 37 X

Jack and the Beanstalk

Barbara Vagnozzi

Child's Play (2004) HB £5.99
ISBN: 0 85953 676 9

Here are two delightfully amusing versions of this classic tale. When hard times come to Jack and his mother, she reluctantly decides that they must sell their cow, Daisy. Jack is entrusted with taking the cow to market but things don't quite go according to plan when Jack exchanges Daisy for a handful of 'magic beans' instead! Richard Walker's retelling, combined with Niamh Sharkey's distinctive, humorous illustrations, make this a fun picture book to share. Barbara Vagnozzi's lift-the-flap version leaps to life with its rich colour; children will really enjoy working their way through this book and finding the surprise under each flap. Look out for other books in this series – *Goldilocks and the Three Bears, Little Red Riding Hood* and *The Three Little Pigs.*

The Story Tree: Tales to Read Aloud

Hugh Lupton
illustrated by Sophie Fatus

Barefoot (2004) PB £8.99
ISBN: 1 84148 627 2

This jolly anthology of folk tales contains seven traditional stories from many parts of the world. *The Magic Porridge Pot* is an old German favourite from Grimm's Fairy Tales, and *The Sweetest Song* is an old American Black folk tale. There is a Jewish story about a boy without a coat, a Russian story and an Indian tale, as well as the very traditional *The Three Billy Goats Gruff*

Did you know?

Jack and the Beanstalk ***was made into a film in 1952 starring Abbott and Costello***

Folk & Fairy Tales

and *The Little Red Hen*. This charming collection is gloriously illustrated by French artist Sophie Fatus, who graduated from the Academy of Fine Art in Paris in 1980. *The Story Tree* is also available as an unabridged audio book, narrated by Hugh Lupton.

The Dragon's Tears

Manju Gregory
illustrated by Guo Le

Mantra (2001) PB £7.50
ISBN: 1 85269 700 8

This folk tale comes from China and tells the story of how the twenty-four lakes of the River Min got the name 'The Dragon's Tears'. When Chun Li releases a golden fish that he has caught, he is rewarded with the gift of a magic pearl. This pearl has the ability to multiply everything that it is placed against. For his mother and Chun Li, this means an end to their poverty and hunger. But with this gift, Chun Li's troubles really begin. This is a moving story, sensitively told by Manju Gregory, and Guo Le's Chinese brush art illustrations are lively and full of energy. A dual language book, this edition is in Vietnamese and English.

Cunning Cat Tales

Laura Cecil
illustrated by
Emma Chichester Clark

Chrysalis (2004) PB £6.99
ISBN: 1 84365 023 1

This is a collection of three stories about cats: the well-known *Puss in Boots*; the lesser known *The White Cat*, a seventeenth-century French fairy tale by Madam d'Aulnoy; and *Sir Pussycat*, from an Italian folk tale, *Il Gatto Mammone* similar to the better-known *Diamonds and Toads* by Perrault. Meet the cat with the red boots whose cunning brings his master riches, a castle and a beautiful princess; the sleek, beautiful white cat who lives in a castle encrusted with precious stones and walls made of crystal, who helps a young prince to fulfil his father's challenge; and finally, Sir Pussycat who helps a young girl to escape the life of misery that has been inflicted upon her by her cruel mother and selfish sister. This collection is ideal for reading aloud, giving the reader plenty of opportunity to use different voices and to repeat phrases so that children can join in. Emma Chichester Clark's vivid illustrations, rich in colour and drama, bring these feline creatures alive.

Wicked Wolf Tales

Laura Cecil
illustrated by
Emma Chichester Clark

Pavilion (2003) PB £6.99
ISBN: 1 84365 018 5

This anthology contains three tales about wolves: *Little Red Riding Hood*, *The Wicked Wolf and the Seven Little Kids* will be familiar to many readers, but the final tale, *Mr W. Wolf*, is less well known. It is a humorous Italian folktale about a young girl who loves doughnuts so much that she plays a trick on Mr Wolf. Instead of giving him the doughnuts her mother prepares for him, she decides to eat them all up. Emma Chichester Clark's illustrations are the perfect choice to accompany this highly dramatic and humorous retelling.

Folk & Fairy Tales

No Dinner! The Story of the Old Woman and the Pumpkin

Jessica Souhami

Frances Lincoln (2000) PB £5.99
ISBN: 0 7112 1459 X

This is a popular folk tale from the Indian subcontinent. A frail old woman sets out to visit her granddaughter who lives in the forest. Her journey is fraught with danger as she encounters a selection of fierce and hungry animals – a wolf, a bear and a tiger – who want to eat her. By a clever means of deception she manages to persuade them that she will taste even better if they wait until after she has eaten her dinner! Jessica Souhami's adaptation of this tale possesses a strong theatrical mood throughout. There is a perfect synchrony of pictures and text, which will make children – and adults – want to revisit this tale again and again.

Rama and the Demon King: An Ancient Tale from India

Jessica Souhami

Frances Lincoln (1998) PB £5.99
ISBN: 0 7112 1158 2

This ancient tale dates back 3,000 years and was passed orally from person to person until the poet Valmiki wrote it down in the Ramayana. It tells of how Rama rescued his wife, Sita, from the Demon ten-headed King Ravana. Jessica Souhami's retelling conveys the exuberance of this tale, and her stunning and beautifully executed illustrations – adapted from her own shadow puppets – bring the vibrant colours and beauty of India alive. Almost every region of India has its own version of this story; Souhami's short version is a perfect introduction to a legendary tale for younger children.

The Emperor's New Clothes

Marcus Sedgwick
illustrated by Alison Jay

Templar (2004) HB £9.99
ISBN: 1 84011 842 3

The Emperor's New Clothes

Eve Tharlet, translated by Rosemary Lanning

North-South Books (2002) PB £4.99
ISBN: 0 7358 1701 4

Here are two ingenious retellings of one of Hans Christian Andersen's funniest tales, which first appeared in 1836 and was translated into English in 1846. It is a satirical story of a very vain Emperor who adores beautiful new clothes and has wardrobes full of them! When two sly swindlers, masquerading as weavers, tell him that they can make the most beautiful cloth he has ever seen into an incredible outfit, the Emperor's foolhardy vanity gets the better of him. Marcus Sedgwick's retelling is masterfully accomplished. He has used verse to enhance the text and animals to give an anthropomorphic and humorous account of this story. Alison Jay's illustrations are of a stunning quality and they beautifully accompany the written text. Eve Tharlet's adaptation of the same story has an eighteenth-century setting and has been illustrated with soft, colourful watercolours.

Folk & Fairy Tales

Little Red Riding Hood

Josephine Evett-Secker
illustrated by
Nicoletta Ceccoli

Barefoot (2004) HB £10.99
ISBN: 1 84148 619 1

Little Red Cap

Translated from German by
Elizabeth D. Crawford
illustrated by Lisbeth Zwerger

North-South Books (1995) PB £3.99
ISBN: 1 55858 430 7

This much-loved fairy tale was first told by Charles Perrault and later by the Brothers Grimm. It is a story of innocence and trust that contains a darker element. When Little Red Riding Hood/Little Red Cap sets out into the forest to visit her grandmother, she meets a cunning wolf who befriends her but all the while is planning to have her for his next meal! Josephine Evetts-Secker's lively retelling of *Little Red Riding Hood* sparkles with detail, while retaining the original essence of the story. The breathtaking, colourful pencil and oil pastel illustrations by Nicoletta Ceccoli portray an enchanting Little Red Riding Hood together with a wonderfully enticing wolf! *Little Red Cap*, translated from the German by Elizabeth Crawford, is accompanied with illustrations by award-winning illustrator Lisbeth Zwerger that bring out the humour in this tale. Little Red Cap appears winsome and naughty while the wolf is portrayed as beguiling.

Peter and the Wolf

Sergei Prokofiev
illustrated by Julia Gukova
Adapted by Gerlinde Wiencirz
Translated by Anthea Bell

North-South Books (1999) HB £9.99
ISBN: 0 7358 1188 1

Peter and the Wolf

Pie Corbett
illustrated by Nik Pollard

Chrysalis (2004) HB £10.99
ISBN: 1 85602 462 8

Sergei Prokofiev's symphonic fairy tale for narrator and orchestra was written in 1939 and has enchanted young readers for many years. Peter, a young boy, lives with his grandfather in a house in the middle of the forest. Although Peter is warned by his grandfather of the existence of a dangerous and hungry wolf in the forest, Peter's curiosity gets the better of him. When he sees the wolf chasing the fat duck, little bird and old tabby cat he devises a clever plan to trick the wolf. Julia Gukova's version is aimed at an older audience and her illustrations are spectacular with a strong European flavour. The Pie Corbett version is a novelty book with incredible pop-ups that will entertain children for hours – especially of the hungry wolf in the middle of the book!

Did you know?

Charles Perrault saw his tale **Little Red Riding Hood** *as a warning to children not to talk to strangers*

Folk & Fairy Tales

The Pied Piper of Hamelin

Robert Browning
illustrated by André Amstutz

Orchard (1994) PB £5.99
ISBN: 1 85213 6510

The Pied Piper

Henriette Barkow
illustrated by Roland Dry

Mantra (2002) PB £7.50
ISBN: 1 85269 975 2

The Pied Piper of Hamelin features the unabridged version of the celebrated narrative poem for children by Robert Browning. Based on a story originally dating back to the thirteenth-century about the town of Hamelin in Germany, it tells of how the town is plagued with an infestation of rats. When an oddly dressed stranger appears in their midst offering his help, the Mayor and Corporation accept immediately. Known as the Pied Piper, he possesses an extraordinary skill that he uses to great effect to rid the town of their rats. The narrative is beautifully complemented by the striking illustrations of André Amstutz. Sumptuous in colour and detailed in characterisation, they capture a real sense of Hamelin in medieval times. Henriette Barkow's *The Pied Piper* – a dual language book in both Polish and English – is sensitively retold and the bright, vibrant illustrations by Roland Dry accompany the narrative perfectly. Available in 22 different languages, this wonderful tale can be shared throughout the world.

The Faery's Gift

Tanya Robyn Batt
illustrated by Nicoletta Ceccoli

Barefoot (2003) HB £10.99
ISBN: 1 84148 997 2

This tale comes from the Isle of Cape Clear, off the coast of Southern Ireland; it is a clever, magical story of Faery ingenuity and the human spirit of generosity. A poor woodcutter lives with his wife, father and mother in a small cottage on the edge of a forest. One day, the woodcutter sees a hawk circling its prey and is astonished to discover a faery cowering nearby. He scares the hawk away and is rewarded with the gift of one wish that can be used for anything he desires. He thinks of all the things that he has ever wanted but, when he listens to his family's needs – each wanting something different – the gift soon becomes a burden. This is a beautiful story, enchantingly retold by storyteller Tanya Robyn Batt and accompanied by the glowing, distinctive illustrations of Nicoletta Ceccoli – winner of the prestigious Italian Anderson Prize in 2001 – which help to create a truly spellbinding tale.

The Fox and the Stork: A Fable by Aesop

Karl Rühmann
illustrated by
Alessandra Roberti
translated by Anthea Bell

North-South Books (2003) HB £9.99
ISBN: 0 7358 1809 6

When hungry Stork is invited to share Fox's mouse-tail soup, little does she realise that the cunning creature has no intention of sharing his meal with her. He serves up the soup in a shallow bowl that Stork can't get her beak into, and leaves her to peck uselessly at the liquid. Hiding her displeasure, she determines to get her own back on the nasty Fox, and invites him for dinner the following day... This is not the most exciting fable ever written, but Anthea Bell's translation of Karl Rühman's retelling is lively. In addition, Alessandra Roberti injects humour into her illustrations and depicts both Fox and Stork with gusto and charm.

Little Inchkin

Fiona French

Frances Lincoln (1995) PB £5.99
ISBN: 0 7112 0917 0

This tale from Old Japan is very similar to the Tom Thumb story. Little Inchkin is only as big as a lotus flower, but despite this he has the courage of a Samurai warrior. Against all the odds he is able to prove his valour and win the hand of a princess. It is only then that Lord Buddha grants him his dearest wish. Fiona French's exquisite illustrations are rich in colour and convey a true feeling of Old Japan; in addition, the beautifully illustrated borders add richness to the page. Children will not fail to be enthralled by the Dragon boat or the two fiery demons!

The Glass Garden

Joyce Dunbar
illustrated by Fiona French

Frances Lincoln (2000) PB £5.99
ISBN: 0 7112 1445 X

This tale from Italy is set in the Venice of a bygone age, where glassmaker Lorenzo lives with his family. After his wife tragically dies from a terrible bee sting, he takes his daughter Lucia to live on a rocky island where there are no birds, flowers or bees. He builds her an exquisite glass garden filled with colourful flowers, butterflies and birds but time stands still in the garden and it does not make Lucia happy. When a glass gondola mysteriously appears, Lucia feels powerless to resist its enticement. She is carried away to meet a masked stranger whose gift of a glass rose pierces the heart of her fragile life. Joyce Dunbar, who has produced over 50 children's books, has brought this Venetian tale to life. Fiona French's silhouette illustrations and her striking and boldly coloured page borders give a feeling of eighteenth-century Venice. Children will love the sumptuous display of carnival outfits and masks.

The Princess Mouse: A Tale of Finland

Aaron Shepard
illustrated by Leonid Gore

Simon & Schuster (2003) HB £9.99
ISBN: 0 689 83697 X

The Princess Mouse is a retelling of a classic Finnish folk tale. When the time comes for a farmer's two sons to be married, they have to follow an age-old family tradition. Each son must chop down a tree and whichever way it falls he must go in that direction in search of a bride. While Mikko's brother is artful and makes sure the tree he fells points in his sweetheart's direction, Mikko has to set out into the forest to find a sweetheart of his own. When he does, she is not what he expected! An unusual tale told by Aaron Shepard and complemented by the crayon-like luminous illustrations of Russian illustrator Leonid Gore. These perfectly capture the atmosphere of the dark wood with its various shades of green and blue.

Folk & Fairy Tales

The Princess and the Pea

Dorothée Duntze

North-South Books (1995) PB £4.99
ISBN: 1 55858 381 5

This version of the well-known classic tale by Hans Christian Andersen is simply retold and delicately illustrated by French illustrator Dorothée Duntze. When a prince sets out to find a princess to marry, he wants her to be the 'real thing'. He travels the length and breadth of the world in search of a wife and meets plenty of princesses but none are suitable. One stormy night a princess turns up at the castle and the Queen decides to find out whether she is a real princess or not! Dorothée Duntze has produced intricate and detailed illustrations of haunting faces and unusual scenic perspectives. The pale, warm shades in pastel colours have a distinctive art nouveau style. This large-format book will appeal to children and they will enjoy the humour in this tale.

The Selfish Giant

Oscar Wilde
illustrated by
Katrien van der Grient

Floris (1995) HB £8.99
ISBN: 0 86315 212 0

The Selfish Giant

Oscar Wilde
illustrated by Lisbeth Zwerger

North-South Books (1994) PB £4.99
ISBN: 1 55858 293 2

Oscar Wilde wrote this and other fairy stories for his two young sons, which were published as *The Happy Prince and Other Tales* in 1888. One of his most moving tales, its moral shows how selfishness can lead to great unhappiness. When a Selfish Giant stops a group of children playing in his beautiful garden, spring and summer cease to exist and winter takes over with its snow, frost, hail and strong winds. It is only when the Giant understands the extent of his selfishness – emphasised by the story's mystical ending – that his garden blooms again. Katrien van der Grient's illustrations are colourful with slightly caricatured figures that give the story a contemporary feel. Illustrator Lisbeth Zwerger – winner of the international award for lifetime achievement, the Hans Christian Andersen Medal – has produced a version that by contrast is set in the same century that the story was written. Her striking, delicate watercolour illustrations complement this story beautifully.

The Twelve Dancing Princesses

Jane Ray

Orchard (2002) PB £5.99
ISBN: 1 84121 778 6

One of the best-known Grimm fairy tales has been retold and sumptuously illustrated by Jane Ray. A puzzled King wishes to discover why the silk shoes of his twelve daughters are worn to shreds every morning. He declares that whoever can discover where his daughters go at night will be able to choose one of them to be his wife. First, though, the challenger has to outwit the clever princesses... Jane Ray's exquisitely detailed illustrations, highlighted in gold and silver, and her decorative page borders make this is a beautiful gift edition of a well-loved story.

Folk & Fairy Tales

The Frog Prince

David Lloyd
illustrated by Jan Ormerod

Walker (2002) PB £4.99
ISBN: 0 7445 9414 6

This Brothers Grimm tale about a princess who drops a golden ball into a spring, which is retrieved by a frog who demands in return to eat from her golden plate and sleep on her royal pillow is well known; it is a story of a promise lightly made but reluctantly kept. This attractive lyrical retelling is accompanied by delicate art deco style illustrations that are full of vibrancy and colour.

Snow White and Rose Red

Bernadette Watts

North-South Books (1997) PB £5.50
ISBN: 1 55858 696 2

Snow White and Rose Red live in an isolated cottage in the middle of the forest with their widowed mother. One wintry night there is a knock at the door and they discover a bear standing in the doorway. Invited in to warm himself by the fire, he continues to visit them every evening throughout the winter; when spring arrives, the bear goes on his way. This is not the last that Snow White and Rose Red see of the bear, but in the meantime they have one or two adventures of their own! Bernadette Watts has illustrated several Brothers Grimm and Hans Christian Andersen tales (including *Rumpelstiltskin*, also published by North-South) and is the sole UK participant in the Hans Christian Andersen Bicentennial project. Her vibrant illustrations bring this magical tale to life and allow the humour of the story to unfold. This is a large-format book, which is ideal for reading aloud.

The Children of Lir

Sheila MacGill-Callahan
illustrated by Gennady Spirin

Ragged Bears (2002) PB £6.99
ISBN: 1 85714 128 8

The Children of Lir

Dawn Casey
illustrated by Diana Mayo

Mantra (2003) PB £7.50
ISBN: 1 85269 828 4

Loosely based on an Irish myth, *The Children of Lir* tells the story of a king with twin sons, whose beautiful wife dies giving birth to twin girls. To ease his loneliness, the king marries his sister-in-law, but as time passes and she fails to fall pregnant, she becomes jealous of the children and casts a spell on them, turning them into swans for 'three times three hundred years, or until the Man from the North shall be joined to the Woman from the South'. Sheila MacGill-Callahan's lyrical and spare text is embellished by Gennady Spirin's extraordinarily detailed watercolours, which are given the chance to shine on full-page and double-page spreads. She manages to convey the power, grace and beauty of the swans, but also the anguish of their entrapment, and there is something almost Pre-Raphaelite about the king and his family. Mantra Books also publish a dual language version of this tale in Gujarati and English, retold by Dawn Casey and illustrated by Diana Mayo.

Folk & Fairy Tales

The Wild Swans

Mathew Price
illustrated by
Atsuko Morozumi

Mathew Price Limited (2003)
PB £5.99 ISBN: 1 84248 073 1

Princess Eliza and her eleven brothers live happily in their father's beautiful palace until the arrival of their wicked stepmother. Eliza is banished to the country to live with a peasant family, but her brothers are turned into white swans. As Eliza gets older she longs to find her brothers, and sets out on a dangerous journey to discover their whereabouts. This is a delightful picture book and the colourful illustrations by Atsuko Morozumi capture the magic of this classic tale of faithful love and of happiness lost but finally regained.

Una and the Sea-Cloak

Malachy Doyle
illustrated by Alison Jay

Frances Lincoln (2004) HB £10.99
ISBN: 0 7112 1962 1

Malachy Doyle's story is woven from traditional Irish folk motifs. Martin is astonished when he sees a strange girl staggering out of the sea wearing a tattered green cloak. She is so distressed that Martin takes her home to his mother to see if she can repair Una's garment. However, this is no easy task because they have to search far and wide for the necessary materials – silver grasses, tiny green feathers and rare shells – needed to repair the cloak so that Una can return to her home. This tale, expertly told by Malachy Doyle, evokes an ethereal quality that is perfectly captured by Alison Jay's hauntingly bold and magical illustrations.

The Village that Vanished

Ann Grifalconi
illustrated by Kadir Nelson

Ragged Bears (2002) HB £9.99
ISBN: 1 85714 251 9

This atmospheric and dignified picture book is a story about faith, courage and survival. Told in the style of an African folk teller (called a griot), it demonstrates how knowledge about, and mythology of, ancestors is traditionally passed on from one generation to the next. The story is about young Abikanile and her mother Njemile, who, with the rest of their village, decide to remove all traces of their home and go deeper into the jungle to escape marauding slave traders. Only old Chimwala remains behind, posing as a hermit, to put the evil men off the scent. A combination of Njemile's foresight, Chimwala's bravery and Abikanile's courage saves the villagers from harm. Ann Grifalconi perfectly captures the spirit of the oral folk tale by punctuating her text with exclamation marks and italics, and Kadir Nelson's delicate illustrations beautifully convey the poise of the villagers and the lushness of their jungle home.

The Sorcerer's Apprentice

Inga Moore

Walker (2002) PB £4.99
ISBN: 0 7445 9429 4

Franz's meddling eventually leads his exasperated parents to send him out into the world to find his fortune. Passing a sign – 'Apprentice wanted – apply within' – he decides to try his luck, finding himself at the castle home of a sorcerer. Franz is taken on as the apprentice and is made to work hard,

Folk & Fairy Tales

6-8

but it is not long before he starts meddling again. When he tries out one of his master's magic spells he discovers that he cannot remember how to stop it! This story is probably best known (in adapted form) from *Fantasia*, the Disney film of the 1940s. Written as an accompaniment to the music of the symphonic poem *L'Apprenti Sorcier* by Dukas (1897), the tale was based on an earlier poem by Goethe, but its origins can be traced back even further to the Latin poet Lucian, who was writing in the second century AD. This is a lovely retelling of the story, with humorous, brightly coloured illustrations by Inga Moore.

The Adventures of Tom Thumb

Marianna Mayer
illustrated by Kinuko Y. Craft

SeaStar (2001) HB £9.99
ISBN: 1 58717 064 7

From the magical moment of his birth, Tom Thumb is destined for adventure. He is swallowed by a cow, snatched by a crow, and gulped down by a fish. But even these extraordinary events cannot prepare Tom for the ultimate life-or-death struggle with the formidable giant Gembo who decides that he's had enough of tiny Tom's tenacity! Both Marianna Mayer's lively narrative, driven by the oral storytelling tradition, and Kinuko Craft's astounding paintings, inspired by twelfth-century manuscript illumination, are full of surprise. In this gift edition, one of the most beloved heroes of fairy tale literature is reborn with all of the spirit and drama that has delighted readers for centuries.

Did you know?

Walt Disney produced his first feature-length animated version of* Snow White and the Seven Dwarfs *in 1937

Snow-White

Josephine Poole
illustrated by Angela Barrett

Red Fox (1993) PB £5.99
ISBN: 0 09 918561 X

There have been many versions of this well-known story of Snow White, her wicked stepmother, the magical talking mirror and the seven dwarfs, but this edition is simply breathtaking. Elegantly retold by Josephine Poole, the exquisite illustrations by Angela Barrett are truly stunning and full of atmospheric, haunting appeal. Described in 1993 by the *Sunday Times* as 'the year's best-illustrated classic' this book must surely be considered a classic of children's literature that will endure for many years to come. This really is a book that children of all ages will want to treasure.

Hansel and Gretel

Jane Ray

Walker (1999) PB £5.99
ISBN: 0 7445 6960 5

Hansel and Gretel

Anthony Browne

Walker (2003) PB £4.99
ISBN: 0 7445 9833 8

Folk & Fairy Tales

Hansel and Gretel
Dorothée Duntze
translated by Anthea Bell

North-South Books (2001) HB £10.99 ISBN: 0 7358 1422 8

The dark tale of the two children, abandoned by their parents in the forest, and their frightening encounter with an evil witch, has lost none of its popularity over the years; each of these versions is testament to its appeal. Jane Ray's straight retelling of this story, and her exquisite, glittering illustrations (the pink gingerbread house, and the gold flecks that light up the night-time forest) display her luminous and intricate style. Anthony Browne's *Hansel and Gretel*, adapted from the translation by Eleanor Quarrie (1949), has a distinctly contemporary feel, which the humorous illustrations enhance (the woodcutter, for example, has a television set in his home, and the cruel stepmother, a cigarette hanging from her mouth, trips daintily along in high heels and a striking yellow coat), bringing an element of humour to this dark tale. In contrast, Dorothée Duntze's version is more traditional and ideal for reading aloud. Her illustration of the witch is truly terrifying!

The Bee-Man of Orn
Frank R. Stockton
illustrated by P. J. Lynch

Walker (2003) HB £12.99
ISBN: 0 7445 9612 2

This unusual and interesting American story first appeared in 1887 in Stockton's collection *The Man of Orn and Other Fanciful Tales.* It is about an old man who lives alone in a cottage, surrounded by bees and existing on honeycomb. One day, a young sorcerer puts forward the notion that the Bee-Man has been transformed from something else; determined to find out just what he may have been originally, he straps a hive to his back and sets off into the world. After many adventures, it transpires that the old man had once been … a baby, into which the sorcerer promptly changes him back. Many years pass, and he grows up once more … into a Bee-Man! P. J. Lynch's illustrations for this odd tale about destiny are sublime: the honeyed tones of the old man's cottage; the verdant lushness of the valleys through which he travels; the forbidding grey-greens of the caves into which he descends; and the fierce orange of the fire-breathing dragon from which he rescues a baby are all dramatically and beautifully realised. It is a stunning adaptation of a curious story.

Sleeping Beauty
Mahlon F. Craft
illustrated by Kinuko Y. Craft

SeaStar (2002) HB £9.99
ISBN: 1 58717 120 1

Sleeping Beauty
Adèle Geras
illustrated by
Christian Birmingham

Scholastic (2003) HB £14.99
ISBN: 0 439 98145 X

These two enchanting editions of a well-known Charles Perrault fairy tale will appeal to children and adults alike. Kinuko Y. Craft's stunning illustrations have a strong Pre-Raphaelite flavour (particularly the illustration showing Sleeping Beauty being awakened by the Prince's kiss) and reflect the true spirit of the tale. Acclaimed author Adèle

Folk & Fairy Tales

Geras has woven her own brand of magic into this tale beautifully. The artwork by talented illustrator Christian Birmingham perfectly complements the text with his atmospheric soft-pastel technique. There are some stunning full-page colour plates, as well as many black and white sketches throughout that sparkle with enchantment and are sure to capture the imaginations of a new generation of children.

Cinderella
Kinuko Y. Craft

SeaStar (2000) HB £9.99
ISBN: 1 58717 004 3

This 'rags-to-riches' story is one of the most well-known and best-loved fairy tales. Kinuko Y. Craft has set this adaptation in seventeenth- and eighteenth-century France. The dresses are voluminous confections of ribbons and pink satin, the hairstyles curled and flowing, and the palace gaudy with chandeliers. It is a somewhat cloying, romantic and traditional vision, but in some ways it suits the royal theme of the story well. The text, in this case adapted from Arthur Rackham and Andrew Lang rather than Charles Perrault, is surrounded by intricately designed borders and decorated with designs that become more elaborate as the story unfolds.

The Fisherman & His Wife
John Howe

Creative Editions (2001) HB £10.99
ISBN: 1 56846 140 2

One day, a poor fisherman catches a fish; when the fish pleads with him to let him go, he puts him back in the sea. As a reward, the fish grants the man a number of wishes. Goaded on by his avaricious wife, the fisherman is forced to constantly ask for more and more, until the woman's greed goes too far and she finds her final, preposterous wish answered in a most unusual way. John Howe, a renowned Tolkien artist, whose paintings have been used for the covers of *The Hobbit* and *The Lord of the Rings* books, has produced a variety of stunning aquatic images that balance the reality and fantasy of this classic tale.

The Steadfast Tin Soldier
Georges Lemoine

Creative Editions (2002) HB £10.99
ISBN: 1 56846 142 9

This classic, bittersweet Hans Christian Andersen story of unfulfilled love will entrance readers of all ages. When a set of tin soldiers is made, one of them is left incomplete, without a leg. Nevertheless, he remains stoical and falls in love with a pretty paper Dancer, who he dreams will one day become his wife. But when a terrible mishap occurs, he find himself embarking on a dangerous journey that will test his bravery to the utmost. He is finally united with his beloved Dancer in a manner which is both tragic and fitting. French artist Georges Lemoine has illustrated more than 60 picture books; his striking pictures capture the story's true essence, bringing it vividly to life.

Did you know?

The earliest European* Cinderella *tale was published in Italy and was known as* La Gatta Cenerentola *(The Hearth Cat)

Folk & Fairy Tales

The Sleeping Princess and other Fairy Tales from Grimm

Saviour Pirotta
illustrated by
Emma Chichester Clark

Orchard (2002) HB £12.99
ISBN: 1 84121 541 4

The Sleeping Princess is a collection of ten stories by the Brothers Grimm retold with humour by Saviour Pirotta. Included here are well-known favourites – *The Golden-Haired Girl in the Tower* (the story of Rapunzel); *The Naughty Princess and the Frog* (The Frog Prince); and *The Girl Who Spun Straw into Gold* (Rumpelstiltskin), and some lesser-known tales, such as *The Little Mouse and the Lazy Cat.* Emma Chichester Clark's illustrations, with their rich, glowing colours, vividly capture the atmosphere of enchanting interiors and mysterious deep, dark forests alike.

Elf Hill: Tales from Hans Christian Andersen

Naomi Lewis
illustrated by
Emma Chichester Clark

Frances Lincoln (2001) PB £7.99
ISBN 0 7112 1830 7

As Naomi Lewis says in her introduction to *Elf Hill*, 'Genius must be the nearest thing to magic that any human being can possess'. Andersen, son of an illiterate peasant woman and a shoemaker, certainly possessed genius in abundance. For *Elf Hill*, Naomi Lewis has chosen nine of his tales, some well-known *(The Princess and the Pea)*, others less so *(Elf Hill; Money-Box Pig* and *Little Ida's Flowers)*, and retold them with the poetic immediacy of an oral storyteller. The language is simple and charming, the typeface large and clear. Emma Chichester Clark's delicate illustrations reflect the author's lightness of touch, depicting sweetly smiling flowers, happy Chinese courtiers, dancing elves, and conspiratorial soft toys. Even the snails have butter-wouldn't-melt expressions. This perfect partnership of author and illustrator has conjured up a marvellous introduction to the amazing world of Andersen.

The Enchanted Gazelle: An African Fairy Tale

Saviour Pirotta
illustrated by Alan Marks

Franklin Watts (2004) HB £8.99
ISBN: 0 7496 5432 5

This handsome hardback book is part of the *Once Upon a World* series, which emphasises our global heritage by bringing together two thematically-similar stories from different parts of the world. Both of the tales in this title are about people who have been helped by clever animals: *The Enchanted Gazelle* is a Swahili story; and *Puss in Boots* is an old favourite. An introduction explains the development of these tales, and there are also ideas for activities, which will be particularly useful for teachers. (The other books in the *Once Upon a World* series are: *Guess My Name* and *Rumpelstiltskin*; *The Glass Palace* and *Sleeping Beauty*; *The Golden Slipper* and *Cinderella*; *The Lonely Princess* and *Rapunzel*; *The Giant Oak Tree* and *Jack and the Beanstalk.*)

Folk & Fairy Tales

My Sister Shahrazad: Tales from the Arabian Nights

Robert Leeson
illustrated by Christina Balit

Frances Lincoln (2003) PB £8.99
ISBN: 0 7112 1767 X

Robert Leeson has collected ten of the best stories from the Arabian Nights including *Aladdin and his Wonderful Lamp* and *Ali Baba and the Forty Thieves*, together with lesser known-tales such as *The Ebony Horse* and the story of *The Lame Young Man and the Barber*. Robert Leeson's masterful adaptations are accompanied by Christina Balit's glorious illustrations, which give a distinct flavour of times gone by and of exotic, far-flung places. A glossary of terms and a list of original sources will prove helpful to young readers.

The Elves and the Shoemaker

Jim La Marche

Chronicle Books (2003) HB £10.99
ISBN: 0 8118 3477 8

An old shoemaker, down on his luck, discovers each morning that wonderful pairs of shoes have been made in his workshop overnight. Finally, he and his wife discover that two tiny elves are responsible. Award-winning artist Jim La Marche's acrylic wash and coloured pencil watercolours bring to life this fine old tale in a manner suited more to the times when the tale was first told.

Cinderella and The Sleeping Beauty

Rose Impey
illustrated by Peter Bailey

Orchard (2001) PB £3.99
ISBN: 1 84121 574 0

The Emperor's New Clothes and The Tinder Box

Andrew Matthews
illustrated by Peter Bailey

Orchard (2001) PB £3.99
ISBN: 1 84121 663 1

Thumbelina and The Tin Soldier

Andrew Matthews
illustrated by Peter Bailey

Orchard (2001) PB £3.99
ISBN: 1 84121 671 2

These three titles are part of the *Orchard Fairy Tales* series and have been illustrated by Peter Bailey, one of the masters of black-and-white illustration. Written and produced in the style of a paperback novel, the stories are printed in a bold and balanced typeface and decorated with exquisite line drawings on every page; this makes them ideal for any child who is just starting to develop confidence as a new reader. (There are many other titles in the series: *The Little Matchgirl* and *The Wild Swans*, *The Little Mermaid* and *The Princess and the Pea*, *Rapunzel* and *Rumpelstiltskin*, *Jack and the Beanstalk* and *The Three Wishes*.)

Folk & Fairy Tales

Enchantment: Fairy Tales, Ghost Stories and Tales of Wonder

Kevin Crossley-Holland
illustrated by
Emma Chichester Clark

Orion (2000) HB £9.99
ISBN: 1 84255 032 2

Kevin Crossley-Holland is an assiduous collector and compiler of old tales from the British Isles. This book (which comprises a selection of stories previously published in other anthologies, and is decorated most charmingly by Emma Chichester Clark) gives us the opportunity to enjoy once more some of our islands' best – but ironically perhaps not best known – tales. Almost all children, for example, can recite the story of *Rumpelstiltskin*, but how many know the very similar *Tom Tit Tot*? Other tales are distinctly cautionary in nature: Gwyn loses his beautiful wife after striking her for the third time; a fisherman is captivated by a sea-woman and takes her sealskin so that she is forced to live on the land with him until the day she manages to escape; and greedy Jack Madden ends up with two humps rather than one when he tries to outwit the fairies (this is the famous Irish story *Lusmore*). Kevin Crossley-Holland's poetic and careful way with words ('his last inch of whisky glowed like molten honey in the flickering firelight') brings these stories beautifully to life.

The Hutchinson Treasury of Fairy Tales

Foreword by Naomi Lewis

Hutchinson (1999) HB £19.95
ISBN: 0 09 176793 8

This anthology of fairy tales has been edited to appeal to as wide a readership as possible. The *Once Upon a Time* section contains stories that are suitable for reading aloud to the under 6s (*Little Red Riding Hood*, *Jack and the Beanstalk*, *Henny Penny*), while two other sections – *When Dreams Came True* and *Long Ago and Far Away* – cater to older readers. Some of the best children's book illustrators (Tony Ross, Shirley Hughes, Quentin Blake and Angela Barrett among them) have been commissioned to produce stunning pictures for this handsome volume.

The Classic Tales of Hans Christian Andersen

Margaret Clark
illustrated by
Christian Birmingham

Scholastic (2002) HB £14.99
ISBN: 0 439 98257 X

Hans Christian Andersen Fairy Tales

Selected and illustrated by
Lisbeth Zwerger
translated by Anthea Bell

North-South Books (2001) HB £15.00
ISBN 0 73581 394 9

Folk & Fairy Tales

Favourite Tales from Hans Christian Andersen

Illustrated by Anastasiya Archipova

Floris (2001) HB £12.99
ISBN 0 86315 347 X

Andersen wrote plays, poetry, novels and travel books, but of course he is remembered primarily for his fairy tales, which have been published in innumerable editions and illustrated in a wide variety of styles all over the world. This diversity is reflected in the three selections under review. Lisbeth Zwerger was appropriately awarded the prestigious Hans Christian Andersen Medal for Illustration in 1990 while working on her selection of Andersen fairy tales. Whether or not this inspired her to reach new heights of creativity is unknown, but the result is quite simply a stunningly beautiful book, immaculately designed and produced. Bell's new translation has given the stories a freshness that imbues them with a feel of nineteenth-century European storytelling, and perfectly reflects Zwerger's exquisite watercolours. This really is a book for fairy tale lovers of all ages, but if the quantity of text is off-putting for younger readers, they could do worse than Floris Books's *Favourite Tales*, which duplicates some of the stories in Zwerger's selection, but breaks up the text with Archipova's plentiful, more traditional, illustrations. Archipova's artwork shares some characteristics with Christian Birmingham's, although the latter works primarily in pastels. His trademark illustrations – in colour and black-and-white – adorn Margaret Clark's retellings in *The Classic Tales*, and will not disappoint his many admirers.

Hidden Tales from Eastern Europe

Antonia Barber
illustrated by Paul Hess
edited by Shena Guild

Frances Lincoln (2003) PB £6.99
ISBN: 0 7112 2118 9

These seven little-known folk tales from Eastern Europe have been poetically retold by Antonia Barber. Here are stories from Russia, Slovenia, Poland, Slovakia, Croatia, Serbia and Romania. Some contain a moral: *The Most Beautiful Flower*, from Slovenia, is about a king who banishes all the old people from his lands only to discover that he has lost all their wisdom; *The Shepherd King*, from Serbia, is about a king who learns how to be humble. There are darkly humorous tales as well, like *Misery*, from Poland, about a poor man and his wife who live with 'misery' until he is successfully banished from their lives; or *The Happy Man*, a tale from Croatia, about a king who yearns for immortality and attempts to solve its riddle. Paul Hess's unusual, atmospheric and dramatic illustrations help to bring these stories alive.

Did you know?

Charles Dickens once confessed that Little Red Riding Hood was his first love, while he bitterly deplored the cruelty and treachery of the disguised Wolf

Folk & Fairy Tales

Tales from Old Ireland

Malachy Doyle
illustrated by Niamh Sharkey

Barefoot (2003) PB £8.99
ISBN: 1 84148 279 X

In the introduction to this enchanting collection, Malachy Doyle states that 'Irish folk tales have a magic and a simplicity, a depth and a passion that appeal to people of all ages and nationalities.' With this in mind, he has embraced the stories' origins in the oral tradition by retelling them with verve and wit, in the hope that they will be read aloud. The only drawback to this for the listener would be missing the utterly marvellous illustrations by Niamh Sharkey, which are visually breathtaking in their composition and originality. They are also very funny. This is a sparkling, wonderful book worthy of a place in anybody's fairy tale library.

The Fabrics of Fairy Tale: Stories Spun from Far and Wide

Tanya Robyn Batt
illustrated by Rachel Griffin

Barefoot (2000) HB £14.99
ISBN: 1 84148 060 6

This unusual book brings together seven stories in which fabric – in some form – plays an integral part. In an Armenian tale, Anaeet the shepherd's daughter only agrees to marry the Prince if he learns a trade; his newly-acquired ability to weave carpets subsequently saves his life. In *The Patchwork Coat* (a Jewish story), Khaim Yankl leaves his family to make his fortune, sewing the money he makes into patches on his coat, only for his wife to give the old garment to a beggar upon his return. A Swedish story, *The Three Fayes,* is a little like *Rumpelstiltskin* in that a girl who cannot spin flax is unexpectedly helped by three old women, but the price for their work is easily paid. The artwork that accompanies the text is made from a mixture of pieces of fabric and other oddments; in addition, a bibliography and brief historical introductions to the fabrics in the stories provide interesting background information.

Grandmothers' Stories: Wise Woman Tales from Many Cultures

Burleigh Mutén
illustrated by Siân Bailey

Barefoot (1999) HB £12.99
ISBN: 1 901223 77 9

As Burleigh Mutén points out in her introduction, 'the wise woman' in matriarchal societies was respected as a source of knowledge; she was often a healer, teacher and leader of her people. As societies changed, however, the wise woman's importance was relegated, thereafter appearing in folk tales as foolish or wicked. The eight stories featured in this volume, from Senegal, Japan, Russia, Hawaii, Mexico, Ireland, Germany and Sweden, portray the wise woman as benevolent, resourceful and independent. Siân Bailey's striking and highly atmospheric illustrations are a true delight and the perfect choice for this highly readable book.

Stories from the Silk Road

Cherry Gilchrist
illustrated by Nilesh Mistry

Barefoot (1999) HB £12.99
ISBN: 1 901223 21 3

These seven tales will take you on an exotic journey along the ancient trade route between East and West known as the Silk Road. Caravans of travellers – comprising merchants and muleteers, spies and shepherds, priests and pilgrims – follow the Silk Road through mountainous regions and flower-filled valleys, quiet villages and crowded bazaars. The book's narrator is the Spirit of the Silk, who introduces each story, and explains how silk is made. Be transported to Chang'an, the old capital of China, to hear the strange tale of the girl who is transformed into a horse's bride because of her father's rash vow; or to Dunhuang, where the local people describe how their beautiful crescent-shaped lake first appeared in the sands. Nilesh Mistry's intricate illustrations, with their jewel-like colours, enhance the stories. The book also contains a useful map outlining the route of the Silk Road, a 'Did you Know' section and a list of sources.

Aladdin and the Enchanted Lamp

Philip Pullman
illustrated by Sophy Williams

Scholastic (2004) HB £14.99
ISBN: 0 439 96298 6

Aladdin and Other Tales from the Arabian Nights

Illustrated by W. Heath Robinson and others

Everyman's Library (1997) HB £9.99
ISBN: 1 85715 912 8

The story of Aladdin is well known throughout the world and has been retold and adapted countless times. It was originally one of a group of tales known as *The Arabian Nights Entertainment* or *The Thousand and One Nights*, which were told by Shahrazad to her husband night after night in an attempt to preserve her life. As Philip Pullman says in the introduction to *Aladdin and the Enchanted Lamp*, his new version of the tale, 'It's got everything: comedy, drama, fantasy, magic, fear, excitement and a terrific plot.' Pullman is a consummate storyteller, and he manages to bring alive this wonderful story in a powerful way. Sophy Williams plays her part by contributing illustrations that add terrific atmosphere and drama. *Aladdin and Other Tales from the Arabian Nights* is a rich and densely written volume, aimed at confident readers; in addition to *Aladdin*, this classic volume also includes *Ali Baba and the Forty Thieves, The Seven Voyages of Sinbad the Sailor*, and five other well-known tales. The illustrations, first published in 1899, are by William Heath Robinson, who was in his twenties when he was commissioned to illustrate a collection of stories from *The Arabian Nights*.

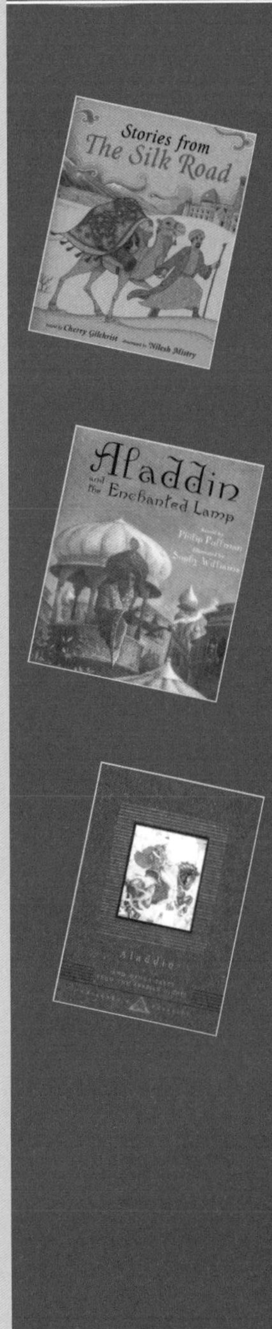

Folk & Fairy Tales

The Barefoot Book of Animal Tales from Around the World

Naomi Adler
illustrated by Amanda Hall

Barefoot (2002) PB £7.99
ISBN: 1 84148 942 5

Amanda Hall's vivid paintings bring to life this selection of nine stories from Brazil, Canada, Kenya, Thailand, Germany, Australia, China, India and the USA. Spiders, rabbits, dragons, frogs and many other creatures feature in these tales, which have been collected by the author on her many travels around the world.

The Nightingale

Stephen Mitchell
illustrated by Bagram Ibatoulline

Walker (2003) PB £6.99
ISBN: 0 7445 9840 0

The Nightingale

Illustrated by Lisbeth Zwerger
translated by Anthea Bell

North-South Books (1999) PB £4.99
ISBN: 0 7358 1120 2

Here are two excellent versions of this well-known tale by Hans Christian Andersen. In the first, Stephen Mitchell has tried to be as faithful to the spirit of the original text as possible. Bagram Ibatoulline's extraordinarily detailed illustrations convey the beauty of Chinese art with rich colours that bring the world of the Emperor of China vividly to life. Anthea Bell's translation of *The Nightingale* from the original Danish is accompanied by Lisbeth Zwerger's exquisite ink and wash drawings, which also conjure up a sensitive, yet powerful, image of ancient China.

The Tale of Tales

Tony Mitton
illustrated by Peter Bailey

David Fickling (2003) HB £12.99
ISBN: 0 385 60517 X

A group of animals travel from the jungle to Volcano Valley to hear the greatest story ever: The Tale of Tales. To pass the time on the long journey, the animals tell their own stories in verse. These are mainly re-workings of old favourites such as *Rip Van Winkle* and the *Anansi* tales. Each tale is linked by prose to form a wonderful collection of stories, which is handsomely decorated with stunning and atmospheric black-and-white line drawings. Peter Bailey has chosen to illustrate the prose and verse sections of the books in different styles, which adds dramatically to the richness and depth of the book.

Rocking Horse Land and Other Classic Tales of Dolls and Toys

Compiled by Naomi Lewis
illustrated by Angela Barrett

Walker (2000) HB £12.99
ISBN: 0 7445 5566 3

These stories were originally published in *The Silent Playmate* (Gollanz, 1979). Hans Christian Andersen's classic tale *The Steadfast Tin Soldier* is an obvious inclusion, but other stories are less familiar: Mrs Fairstar's *The Memoirs of a London Doll* describes a doll's life from the moment she is manufactured by Mr Sprat and his family to her acquisition by a nice girl; Ruth Ainsworth's *Rag Bag* is magical and witty; *Vasilissa, Baba Yaga and the Little Doll* is a Russian fairy tale that has much in common with Cinderella;

Folk & Fairy Tales

Laurence Houseman's *The Rocking Horse Land*, which was first published in 1894, retains its freshness and vitality today; and *The Town in the Library*, a short story by E. Nesbit, captures the joys of childhood games and imagination.

Classic Fairy Tales to Read Aloud

Selected by Naomi Lewis
illustrated by Jo Worth

Kingfisher (2002) PB £5.99
ISBN: 0 7534 0287 4

The fairy tales in this collection have been especially selected for reading aloud. A time has been allocated to each story, lasting from three to thirty minutes. Naomi Lewis is an international authority on the subject of fairy tales; she has written a poignant introduction to this volume, inviting readers to love and believe in the powerful message of fairy tales. She has also translated some of the Hans Christian Andersen stories that are featured here. In this volume you will find well-known tales by Andersen, Charles Perrault and the Brothers Grimm, but also examples of contemporary or unknown ones, such as *Tomkin and the Three Legged Stool* by Vivian French, *The Boy Who Read Aloud* by Joan Aiken or *The Woman of the Sea* by Helen Waddell. Each tale also has a short introduction that helps to understand the story and to place it in its historical context. Overall this is a magnificent collection that children and adults will want to read again and again.

The Thistle Princess and Other Stories

Vivian French
illustrated by Chris Fisher

Walker (1996) PB £3.50
ISBN: 0 7445 4747 4

Vivian French's original fairy stories – *The Thistle Princess*, *Little Beekeeper* and *Tomkin and the Three Legged Stool* – vividly bring to life memorable characters and magical events. A small thistle, alone among the many beautiful flowers in the garden of a childless king and queen, finds the wisdom and courage to help them; the contrasting fortunes of the Little Beekeeper and her rude and foolish older brothers are both satisfying and amusing; and Tomkin the tailor learns a hard lesson when he fails to keep a promise to his magical three-legged stool. Chris Fisher's black and white illustrations are humorous and complement Vivian French's consummate storytelling.

The Mousehole Cat

Antonia Barber
illustrated by Nicola Bailey

Walker (1993) PB £5.99
ISBN: 0 7445 2353 2

Mousehole is a small fishing village in Cornwall, so named because of its small harbour. One winter, the 'Great Storm-Cat' visits the coast, preventing any of the fishing boats from leaving harbour. As the town's food supplies dwindle, old Tom and his faithful cat Mowzer decide to brave the storm. Together they defeat the dangers of the sea, bring home the catch and save the villagers. Nicola Bailey's artwork is renowned for her beautiful depictions of cats; in *The Mousehole Cat* her sumptuous illustrations perfectly accompany Antonia Barber's beautiful narrative.

Folk & Fairy Tales

The Snow Queen
Illustrated by P.J. Lynch

Red Fox (1995) PB £5.99
ISBN: 0 09 948641 5

This is a lyrical retelling of one of Hans Christian Andersen's longest and most intricate stories. A wicked troll creates a mirror that distorts everything it reflects. When the mirror is broken into thousands of tiny fragments, some as small as grains of sand, they disperse throughout the world. Splinters get into people's eyes, distorting their vision so that they can only see what is perverted and corrupt. Other people get splinters in their hearts, making them cold and hard like lumps of ice. When Gerda's friend Kay is afflicted by splinters in his eyes and heart, he changes beyond all recognition. Furthermore, Kay is abducted by the beautiful and cruel Snow Queen and taken to her frozen palace; Gerda sets out on a long journey to rescue him. The romantic style of the illustrations is both magical and lavish, yet still manages to convey the darker elements of this story.

Cinderella
Illustrated by
Roberto Innocenti

Creative Editions (2002) HB £10.99
ISBN: 1 56846 130 5

Roberto Innocenti has chosen to set the Cinderella story in 1920s Britain, which gives him ample opportunity to depict the fashions of the day (flapper dresses, spats, little boys in sailor outfits), the architecture of London (Buckingham Palace, the Palace of Westminster), and the humble stone cottage where Cinderella lives with her step-sisters. Roberto Innocenti is a master of accurate period detail, but there are also some playful images to look out for in his drawings (e.g. the statue outside the palace is holding an umbrella). These marvellous illustrations are given the space they deserve in this handsomely designed book, and perfectly complement Charles Perrault's classic version of the story.

The Story Giant
Brian Patten
illustrated by Chris Riddell

Collins (2004) HB £14.99
ISBN: 0 00 711944 5

For over four thousand years, the Story Giant has been collecting stories from around the world, passing them from generation to generation. However, one tale has always eluded him, and as the Giant gets older and more frail, he know that unless he can find it, he will die and all the wonderful stories will be lost forever. When four children from different parts of the world dream their way into his castle, he gathers them together in one shared dream, in the hope that one of them will be able to tell him the final tale. Brian Patten expertly weaves together 50 stories – some traditional and some of his own making – to create a moving and compelling narrative. The text is complemented by Chris Riddell's lively black-and-white line drawings and eight stunning colour plates.

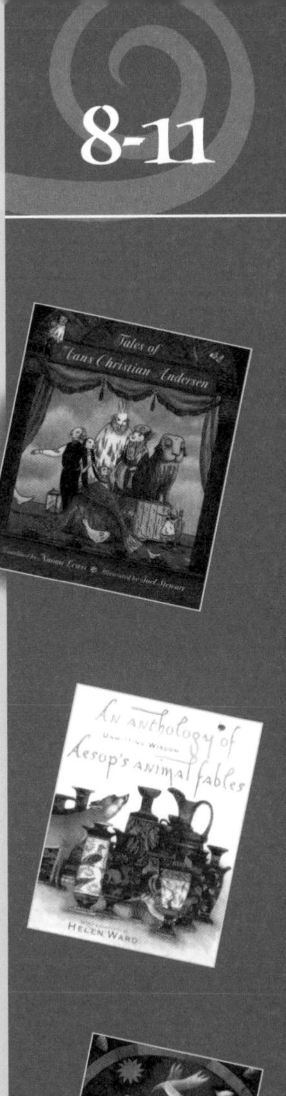

Folk & Fairy Tales

Did you know?

In Copenhagen there is a statue of Hans Christian Andersen's Little Mermaid

Tales of Hans Christian Andersen

Naomi Lewis
illustrated by Joel Stewart

Walker (2004) HB £14.99
ISBN: 0 7445 8895 2

In *Tales of Hans Christian Andersen*, Naomi Lewis has duplicated three of the stories from *Elf Hill* (*The Nightingale, The Princess and the Pea*, and *The Little Match Girl*), with minor changes to the text, but the other ten are new translations. She has also written light-hearted introductions to accompany each tale, explaining how and why Hans Christian Andersen came to write them, and encouraging the reader to think about their meaning. Joel Stewart's colour illustrations are in some ways reminiscent of Emma Chichester Clark's, but his black-and-white bordered drawings are unique and evocative.

Unwitting Wisdom: An Anthology of Aesop's Animal Fables

Helen Ward

Templar Books (2004) HB £14.95
ISBN: 1 84011 429 0

Aesop's fables are characterised by their animal protagonists, but the feelings, desires and dilemmas they face are clearly very human. As a result, each tale is summed up by a concluding moral. Helen Ward's book has been designed to the highest standard: the typesetting, outstanding use of colour and good quality paper all contribute to the success of this marvellous collection.

When the World Began: Stories Collected in Ethiopia

Elizabeth Laird

Oxford University Press (2001)
PB £7.99 ISBN: 0 19 274189 6

These tales were gathered together by Elizabeth Laird as part of the British Council in Ethiopia's story-collecting project, which was funded by the Department for International Development. As Elizabeth Laird explains, 'in Ethiopia great treasuries of stories still live in people's heads and have never been written down'. The diverse nature of Ethiopia, and the different faiths and cultures of its people, are reflected in these tales, which highlight contrasting ideas of God, heaven and the spiritual world. These wise and funny stories are about hunters and animals, cunning and trickery, and love and goodness. They are beautifully illustrated by Yosef Kebade, Emma Harding, Grizelda Hoderness and Lydia Monk.

Folk & Fairy Tales

Dwarf Nose

Wilhelm Hauff
illustrated by Lisbeth Zwerger

North-South Books (1994) HB £9.99
ISBN: 1 55858 261 4

This nineteenth-century German fable was written by a young man who was considered to be a literary genius in his short lifetime (he died at the age of 24). *Dwarf Nose* is the story of Jacob, the son of a vegetable seller, who is turned into a squirrel by an old enchantress and made to work in her home for seven years. One day, while working in her kitchen, he inhales the scent of a particular herb and is transformed into a dwarf with an extremely long nose. A job as a chef in the Duke's kitchen and an acquaintance with a talking goose eventually leads to his retransformation into Jacob and a prosperous life lived happily ever after. There is a lot of text in this book, but Lisbeth Zwerger's divine water-colour illustrations make this edition of an unusual and little-known story very special indeed.

The Clever Rat and Other African Tales

Suzi Lewis-Barned
illustrated by Karen Perrins

Ragged Bears (2002) HB £12.99
ISBN: 1 85714 253 5

Suzi Lewis-Barned's interesting introduction to this colourfully illustrated selection of old East African stories describes how the book came into being. Her father first came across the stories when he was learning Swahili in 1950, in preparation for taking up work in Africa. Upon his return to Britain, he asked friends for books in Swahili, and was sent a collection of stories from which these tales have been selected and retold. Like many of the world's folk tales, these African stories are either cautionary (a dangerous genie released from a bottle; a vain tailor who wants to be rich and powerful), or explain how and why things came to be (why people no longer understand the language of the animals; how the millipede got his legs). The illustrations, on pastel-shaded backgrounds, are bold, bright and colourful, and many of the pages have patterned page borders to enhance the clear and lively text.

The Kingfisher Mini Treasury of Fairy Tales

Vivian French
illustrated by Peter Malone

Kingfisher (2003) HB £6.99
ISBN: 0 7534 0981 X

As Vivian French says in her introduction to this lovely book, 'fairy tales are, surely, the most magical place for a child to go exploring', and this collection is certainly one to treasure. French has revisited some of the traditional tales she heard and read as a child (*Beauty and the Beast, Cinderella, The Elves and the Shoemaker, The Fisherman and His Wife, Hansel and Gretel, Jack and the Beanstalk*, and *Rumpelstiltskin*) and, in addition, has read and re-read as many versions of the stories that she could find, including a seventh-century Chinese Cinderella. She does not claim to offer a faithful or definitive interpretation of any of the stories, but rather has adapted them to be read aloud. Illustrator Peter Malone has created a different world for each fairy tale, bringing them dramatically to life.

Folk & Fairy Tales

Giant Tales from Wales

Brenda Wyn Jones
Illustrated by Peter Brown
translated by Ann Saer

Pont (2003) PB £4.50
ISBN: 1 85902 588 9

What a refreshing collection of tales from Wales this is, poignantly and dramatically narrated with excellent pace and witty dialogue. *The Giant of Snowdonia* is about a nasty giant called Rhitta who spreads terror and bullies the other giants of Snowdonia; feeling very cold one winter's day, Rhitta decides to cut off the other giants' beards so that he can keep himself warm! *The Giant of Pumlumon* has two heads; and the *Giant of the Rhonda* is about Hywel, an argumentative troublemaker. Peter Brown's artwork, both colour and black and white, is beautifully accomplished.

Fairy Tales

Berlie Doherty
illustrated by Jane Ray

Walker (2002) PB £9.99
ISBN: 0 7445 9403 0

This is a collection of favourite traditional stories. Jane Ray's striking illustrations are a perfect accompaniment to the text, which remains true to the more traditional and sometimes grisly versions of the original fairy tales. The book's magnificent full-page illustrations and exquisitely ornate decorative borders are composed of a combination of rich colours and gold leaf. Absolutely beautiful.

Fairy Tales and Fantastic Stories

Terry Jones
illustrated by
Michael Foreman

Chrysalis (2003) HB £14.99
ISBN: 1 84365 055 X

This book was previously published in two separate volumes; *Fairy Tales* deservedly won the 1992 Smarties Award. Terry Jones's original stories in this expanded collection are entertaining and characteristically illustrated in watercolour by Michael Foreman. A number of the tales stand out, in particular *The Ship of Bones*, the story of sailor Bill Stoker who sees the legendary ship of bones, the home of all drowned sailors. He is spirited on to the ship but manages to make his escape by figuring out the one thing that bones might be afraid of. In a wonderful end note, Bill, safely back on his own ship, sits down and eats his own hat!

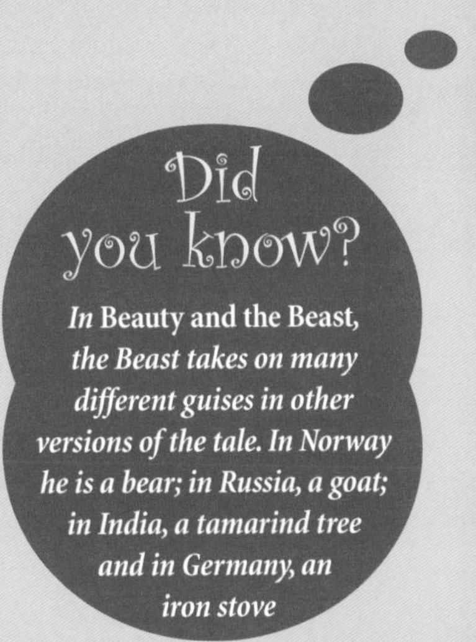

Folk & Fairy Tales

Tales From Grimm

Antonia Barber
illustrated by
Margaret Chamberlain

Frances Lincoln (1998) PB £8.99
ISBN: 0 7112 1341 0

Favourite Grimm's Tales

Illustrated by
Anastasiya Archipova

Floris (2000) HB £12.99
ISBN: 0 86315 318 6

Both of these collections contain a similar selection of all-time favourites – *Snow White*, *Rapunzel* and *Hansel and Gretel* – as well as some lesser-known tales, such as *The Old Man and his Grandson* (a young boy teaches his parents to treat his grandfather with respect) or *The Peasant's Wise Daughter* (a clever peasant girl marries a king). *Tales From Grimm* is a sparkling collection of 15 stories, splendidly retold by Antonia Barber, and beautifully laid out with amusing, delicate watercolour illustrations and brightly coloured borders by Margaret Chamberlain. Floris Books's *Favourite Grimm Tales* contains a selection of 17 stories with illustrations by Anastasiya Archipova that are soft yet vibrant. The layout is ideal for sharing and reading aloud.

Oxford Treasury of Fairy Tales

Geraldine McCaughrean
illustrated by Sophy Williams

Oxford University Press (2003) HB £20.00 ISBN: 0 19 278128 6

The more fairy tales one reads, the more one realises that on the whole they are pretty gruesome little stories. This, of course, is what makes them so appealing, as this marvellous collection amply demonstrates. Geraldine McCaughrean has done a beautiful and witty job of retelling 20 fairy tales, incorporating flashes of light-hearted humour (Farmer Herbert's sons in *The Three Oranges* are called Bigg, Lessor and Scruffy) and touches of menace (Rumpelstiltskin 'gave a hideous cackle and flexed his crackling fingers') into her adaptations. She also manages to finish each story with a memorable and unusual last line, thereby imbuing these age-old tales with fresh resonance. Sophy Williams's gentle illustrations are the perfect accompaniment to Geraldine McCaughrean's words. £20 may seem expensive for a collection of fairy tales, but this attractively designed book will stand the test of time to give pleasure for many, many years.

The Orchard Book of Stories from the Ballet

Geraldine McCaughrean
illustrated by Angela Barrett

Orchard (2003) PB £8.99
ISBN: 1 84362 298 X

Unrequited love, unsuitable wives and cruelty are some of the tragic themes explored in this book. In fact, apart from Cinderella, happy endings are few and far between in Geraldine McCaughrean's retellings, which are not afraid to shy away from the dark themes of the stories . These tales, which include *La Sylphide*, *The Firebird*, *Coppelia*, *Petrouchka*, and *The Nutcracker*, are sensitively illustrated by Angela Barrett (particularly her ethereal depiction of Gisele).

Folk & Fairy Tales

8-11

The Brave Little Tailor

Illustrated by
Sergei Goloshapov
translated by Anthea Bell

North-South Books (1997) HB £9.99
ISBN: 1 55858 634 2

A nimble-fingered tailor sets in motion an incredible chain of events when he swats seven flies in one blow. To commemorate this 'great' feat, he makes a belt, on to which he boldly stitches 'Seven in One Blow'. In true Grimm style, giants, unicorns, wild boars and dishonest kings all fall foul of this nimble hero. The tailor simply believes in himself and manipulates every challenging situation to his advantage. Sergei Goloshapov's bold illustrations convey the dark mood of this larger-than-life folk tale.

The Wonderful Adventures of Nils

Selma Lagerlöf
illustrated by Lars Klinting

Floris (2001) HB £11.99
ISBN: 0 86315 139 6

This is an abridged version of a classic Swedish story first published in two volumes in 1906-7. It tells the story of the adventures of Nil Holgersson, a lazy 14-year-old boy who is changed by an elf into a Tom Thumb-like being. He is taken away by a gander, who flies him all over Sweden until they reach Lapland. Nil's travels give readers the opportunity to learn about Swedish towns, their inhabitants and traditions. This is one of Sweden's best-loved children's books.

The Nutcracker

E.T.A Hoffmann
illustrated by
Lizbeth Zwerger
translated and adapted by
Anthea Bell

Neugebauer Press (1983) HB £6.99
ISBN: 0 907234 33 X

The Nutcracker

E.T.A Hoffmann
illustrated by
Roberto Innocenti

Jonathan Cape (1997) HB £19.99
ISBN: 0 224 04642 X

The story of *The Nutcracker* by E.T.A. Hoffmann was first published in 1819. One Christmas Eve, Herr Drosselmeyer, maker of magical toys, gives his goddaughter Clara a nutcracker. Later that night, Clara creeps downstairs to retrieve it from under the tree, but she falls asleep and is transported into another world, where her nutcracker takes on a human form. When Clara is attacked by the Mouse King, the Nutcracker Prince tries valiantly to defend her but is struck down. Clara in turn saves her Nutcracker Prince by throwing her shoe at the Mouse King. These two editions represent the magnificent work of two of the best children's book illustrators: Roberto Innocenti has been shortlisted several times for the prestigious Hans Christian Andersen Award; and Lisbeth Zwerger has won many prizes for her collectible art. These are two exquisite gift editions to treasure for life.

Folk & Fairy Tales

Swedish Folk Tales

Illustrated by John Bauer
translated by
Holger Lundburgh

Floris (2004) HB £14.99
ISBN: 0 86315 457 3

John Bauer (1882-1918) is one of the world's greatest illustrators of fairy tales. His precise and beautiful work has been compared to that of Dürer and Holbein. This book contains tales about trolls, magicians, princesses, queens, kings and giants by some of the best-known Swedish storytellers (Elsa Beskow, Anna Wahlenberg, Cyrus Granér, Einar Rosenborg and others). Each story reflects the very Swedish folk tradition of describing landscape and the natural environment. This is a book that will appeal equally to both children and adults.

English Fairy Tales

Joseph Jacobs
illustrated by John Batten

Everyman's Library (1993) HB £9.99
ISBN: 1 85715 917 9

This edition contains two volumes, *English Fairy Tales*, which was first published in 1890, and *More English Fairy Tales*, published in 1894. Joseph Jacobs was a folklorist and the editor of a magazine called *FolkLore*; he spent ten years collecting these fairy tales. Jacobs's approach was similar to that of the Brothers Grimm in Germany, but he collected the stories not only from storytellers of the oral tradition but also from printed sources. The 87 tales in this volume cover a wide range of subjects, from animal tales such as *Henny Penny*, to stories of princesses and kings, such as *The King of England and his Three Sons* and *The Princess of Canterbury*.

The Brothers Grimm Fairy Tales

Illustrated by
Arthur Rackham

Everyman's Library (1992) HB £10.99
ISBN: 1 85715 905 5

The Everyman's Library edition of fairy tales by the Brothers Grimm is beautifully decorated by Arthur Rackham (1867-1939), who was commissioned to illustrate these tales in 1900. *Hans in Luck*; *The Twelve Dancing Princesses*; *The Fisherman and His Wife*; *The Frog Prince*; *Rapunzel*; *Tom Thumb* and *Rumpelstiltskin* are just a few of the well-known fairy tales in this book, most of which are told in very short chapters.

Russian Fairy Tales

Gillian Avery
illustrated by Ivan Bilibin

Everyman's Library (1995) HB £9.99
ISBN: 1 85715 935 7

These twelve Russian fairy tales have been retold by a well-known children's book reviewer, historian and authority on the subject. The stories, about princes and princesses, tsars and witches, good against evil, and animals are all strongly rooted in the Russian folk tradition. The illustrations for this gift edition were originally commissioned in 1899 by the Department for the Production of State Documents in Moscow; it took Ivan Bilibin (1876-1942) four years to complete the task.

Folk & Fairy Tales

The Magic Lands: Folk Tales of Britain and Ireland

Kevin Crossley-Holland illustrated by Emma Chichester Clark

Orion (2001) PB £12.99
ISBN: 1 84255 051 9

Kevin Crossley-Holland has thoroughly researched a wealth of stories for this book. In fact, the section of sources and notes at the end of the book is as interesting as the tales themselves, drawing on an established canon of folklore. For instance, the tale of *Tom Tit Tot* comes from Suffolk and is the English counterpart of the Grimms' tale of *Rumpelstilzchen*; *The Small-Tooth Dog from Derbyshire* is a variant of the tale better known as *Beauty and the Beast*. The 55 tales included in this volume reflect the rich heritage of Britain and Ireland's folklore.

The Nightingale that Shrieked and Other Tales

Kevin Crossley-Holland

Oxford University Press (2002)
PB £4.99 ISBN: 0 19 275188 3

This is a most enjoyable collection of stories from Europe, the Middle East and Africa. The title story is an Egyptian tale about a wicked and jealous queen who takes two newborn infants away from their mother, replacing them with a puppy and a water jug instead. In the best tradition of folk tales, however, the victims are eventually reunited with their royal parents. *One Night in Paradise* is a religious tale from Italy about a pledge between two close friends; when one dies, the other goes to paradise to visit him, but on his return he finds that things have tragically changed. This is a compelling collection that children aged 8 to 11 will be able to read by themselves; the concise and easy-to-read stories will also suit reluctant readers. (This is a companion volume to *When the Fish Laughed*, also published by Oxford University Press.)

The Old Stories

Kevin Crossley-Holland illustrated by John Lawrence

Dolphin (1999) PB £5.99
ISBN: 1 85881 753 6

This is a collection of stories from East Anglia and the Fen Country. Kevin Crossley-Holland has chosen short pieces of prose and verse from medieval letters and chronicles, ancient folk beliefs, and extracts from modern diaries and books about the region. One of the most touching stories featured here is *The Suffolk Miracle*, about the love between a poor ploughboy and Rosamund, the daughter of a rich farmer. The farmer opposes their liaison and sends his daughter away; when the ploughboy dies he returns on horseback and carries Rosamund with him to his grave. A useful section on sources and notes, containing fascinating background information about each of the stories, will be particularly useful to anyone who wishes to search out the originals, or to visit some of the places mentioned in these tales. John Lawrence's engravings transport the reader back into the past of this extraordinary landscape.

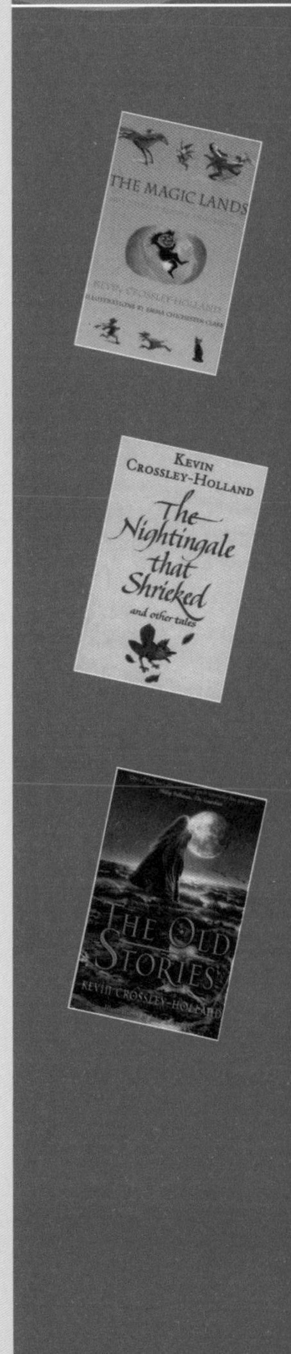

Folk & Fairy Tales

Little Mermaid and Ugly Ducklings

Illustrated by Gennady Spirin

Chronicle Books (2001) HB £13.99
ISBN: 0 8118 1954 X

This beautiful collection is drawn from some of the earliest translations of Hans Christian Andersen's work from his native Danish into English. Six of the most popular Andersen stories – *The Ugly Duckling, Thumbelina, The Steadfast Tin Soldier, The Nightingale, The Princess and the Pea* and *The Little Mermaid* – are included. These are compassionate, wise and funny tales in which the protagonists all learn lessons from their experience of adversity. Russian illustrator Gennady Spirin has produced lavish watercolours in a traditional Renaissance style, which bring these magical stories to life. The book is a bit text-laden and will therefore be more suitable for older readers and adults.

Grimm's Fairy Tales

Illustrated by Arthur Rackham

SeaStar Books (2001) HB £24.99
ISBN: 1 58717 092 2

This is an elegant edition of well-known tales from the Brothers Grimm, complemented by some of Arthur Rackham's classic illustrations. The 22 tales include favourites such as *Rapunzel, Briar Rose, Red Riding Hood, The Goose Girl, Rumpelstiltskin* and *Ashenputtel (Cinderella)*, and lesser-known tales such as *The Water of Life, The Four Clever Brothers, Jorinda and Joringel* and *King Thrushbeard.* Arthur Rackham's colour and black-and-white illustrations are breathtaking: the king with his new born baby daughter in *Briar Rose*; Red Riding Hood as she meets the wolf in the forest and later when she discovers him in her grandmother's bed; and the delicate art deco style of Ashenputtel as she goes to the ball. This is a beautiful book for the whole family to treasure.

Rumpelstiltskin and other Grimm Tales

Carol Ann Duffy, illustrated by Markéta Prachatická

Faber and Faber (1999) PB £8.99
ISBN: 0 571 19631 4

The Stories of Hans Christian Andersen

Diana Crone Frank and Jeffrey Frank

Granta (2004) HB £15.00
ISBN: 1 86207 712 6

This newly-translated selection restores 22 of Hans Christian Andersen's stories to their original glory, removing from them many of the inaccuracies that have accumulated over the last 150 years. The authors have been meticulous in their work, contributing background notes to each story, and an introductory essay that places Andersen in the context of his European literary contemporaries. In common with many recent anthologies of Andersen's work, this book combines some of the better-known stories (*The Princess and the Pea*; *The Red Shoes*) with other lesser-known ones *(By the Outermost Sea*; *Auntie Toothache).* The accompanying illustrations are reproductions of the Danish drawings by Vilhelm Pedersen and Lorenz Frolich, which adorned the original publication; they lend the stories a distinctly Gothic and slightly sinister air that is nevertheless wonderfully appropriate.

Folk & Fairy Tales

Collected Grimm Tales

Carol Ann Duffy
dramatised by Tim Supple

Faber and Faber (2003) PB £9.99
ISBN: 0 571 22142 4

In *Rumpelstiltskin*, the acclaimed poet Carol Ann Duffy retells a selection of tales by the Brothers Grimm in a witty and conversational style. Old favourites are included – *Snow White*, *Rumpelstiltskin*, *Ashenputtel* (an earlier version of *Cinderella)* and *Little Red Cap* while other titles may be new to many readers. In some of the stories the author adds rhythm, while in others, she uses updated slang and humour. *Clever Hans*, for example, is told almost completely in dialogue. All the tales are told here with refreshing disregard for contemporary squeamishness. The witches are unashamedly evil, returning to the darker elements of the original Grimm tales. The poetic language is fresh and vigorous and combines well with the humorous, graphite illustrations by Markéta Prachatická, which add greatly to the spooky mood. These are stories that can be enjoyed by both children and adults.

Collected Grimm Tales contains Carol Ann Duffy's adaptations of Grimm Tales (first published in 1996, Faber) and *More Grimm Tales* (first published in 1997, Faber) as well as a dramatisation by Tim Supple. There are two scripts included: the uncut version of the tales adapted by Carol Ann Duffy for the Young Vic, and the text that was created through rehearsal and performance. The plays were produced by the Young Vic, London, in 1994 and 1997. This is an ideal book for any secondary school library and also for English and Drama Departments.

Puss in Boots, ***first recorded by Charles Perrault, was initially translated from French into English by Robert Samber in 1729, when it was known as*** **The Master Cat.**

Myths & Legends

In this section you will find Greek and Roman myths about gods and goddesses; the legends of King Arthur, Robin Hood and other great heroes; and creation myths from around the world.

Odysseus and the Wooden Horse

Allan Drummond

Orchard (1996) PB £4.99

ISBN: 1 86039 103 6

This famous Greek myth is extracted from Homer's epic poem *The Iliad*, which tells the story of the Trojan war. After many years of battle between the Greeks and the Trojans, Odysseus devises an ingenious plan to outwit the Trojans. He orders the construction of a giant, hollow, wooden horse, which he secretly fills with his soldiers and sends to the Trojans as a gift. When the horse is wheeled into the city of Troy, the Greeks leap to the attack. Allan Drummond has retold and illustrated this exciting story with skill. His images of the soldiers have an authentic Greek feel and his wooden horse is masterfully drawn.

The Kingfisher Treasury of Myths and Legends

Ann Pilling
illustrated by
Kady MacDonald Denton

Kingfisher (2003) PB £8.99

ISBN: 0 7534 0888 0

Ann Pilling has divided this interesting collection of myths and legends from around the world into themed sections (Earth, Air, Fire and Water; Love and Death; Fools and Heroes). A creation myth from West Africa is followed by an Iroquois tale about the four winds; the famous Greek myth of Persephone precedes the less well-known tragic Welsh legend of a prince who mistakenly kills his loyal hound; and the story of Midas and his gold is mirrored by a Russian tale of greed. Norse, Nigerian, Pacific, Irish, Indian, Chinese and English legends are also represented. Numerous watercolour illustrations executed with a lightness of touch accompany and enhance the text.

The Orchard Book of Swords, Sorcerers & Superheroes

Tony Bradman
illustrated by Tony Ross

Orchard (2003) HB £12.99

ISBN: 1 84121 777 8

This collection introduces young readers to some of the world's most famous stories in an accessible form that will hopefully encourage them to seek out the 'originals' later in life. Jason and the Golden Fleece, Aladdin and his Lamp, William Tell, Robin Hood, young King Arthur, Hercules, Ali Baba, George and the Dragon, Theseus and the Minotaur, and Sinbad are all here, rendered with comical twists, modern speech (lots of "er"s, "anyway"s and "right then"s) and accompanied by humorous illustrations. These ancient stories of derring-do offer plenty of opportunity for bold adaptation and Tony Bradman and Tony Ross don't disappoint: Theseus, trembling in front of the Minotaur, says "Prepare to die, foul beast!"; George informs the dragon that he "won't be eating anyone. Not now or ever again"; and Hercules, shortly before despatching the Cacus, tries to placate him by saying "Look, I don't want any trouble." This is knockabout stuff, engaging, witty and addictive.

The Iliad and The Odyssey

Marcia Williams

Walker (1998) PB £5.99

ISBN 0 7445 5430 6

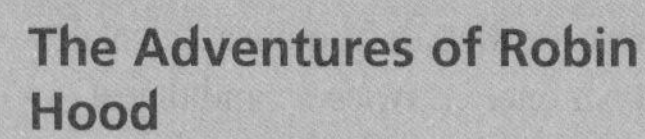

The Adventures of Robin Hood

Marcia Williams

Walker (1996) PB £5.99
ISBN 0 7445 4765 2

King Arthur and the Knights of the Round Table

Marcia Williams

Walker (1997) PB £5.99
ISBN 0 7445 4792 X

Greek Myths for Young Children

Marcia Williams

Walker Books (1994) PB £5.99
ISBN 0 7445 3075 X

Marcia Williams's brilliant wheeze of depicting classic myths and legends in humorous comic-strip format has introduced to very young readers some of the most famous stories, in an accessible and amusing way that is sure to keep them happy for hours. The tales are told in the simplest way possible, in bite-size chunks, but what is really clever is the way the accompanying drawings not only illustrate the words, but also embellish the story. This is particularly effective when Marcia Williams uses speech bubbles, which add an additional layer of entertainment and humour to the books, and allow her to include as much of the story as she can without putting off her audience. The illustrations themselves are wonderfully lively, colourful and packed with little details. A great idea, handsomely executed. (Other retellings to have received the Marcia Williams treatment include *Don Quixote*, *Sinbad the Sailor*, and two volumes about Shakespeare, *Mr William Shakespeare's Plays* and *Bravo, Mr William Shakespeare*.)

The Star-Bearer: A Creation Myth from Ancient Egypt

Dianne Hofmeyr
illustrated by Jude Daly

Frances Lincoln (2002) PB £5.99
ISBN: 0 7112 1663 0

As this beautiful story unfolds it explains, according to Ancient Egyptian belief, how day, night and the starry universe was first created. This ancient story is based on the Heliopolis creation myth, found in the Pyramid Texts dating from 3000 BC, which were preserved in the royal pyramids of the 5th and 6th Dynasties. Dianne Hofmeyr's elegant retelling of this 5,000-year-old myth gives an enchanting explanation of how the godchild Atum begins his work of creation. First he creates the playful gods of air and rain, then Geb, god of the earth and Nut, goddess of the sky. Geb and Nut prove to be inseparable, which leaves Atum no alternative but to force them apart in order than he can continue with his creation. Jude Daly has produced some exquisite illustrations that glow with mystical allure in a recognisable Egyptian style.

The Changeling

Malachy Doyle
illustrated by Jac Jones

Pont (2002) PB £4.95
ISBN: 1 85902 691 5

This perceptive version of a Welsh legend, in which changeling children – human and fairy – fail to thrive in alien environments, but are finally returned to their true families, may be read on many different levels. A young audience will enjoy the fright and reassurance of the story, while older readers (and adults) will recognise that Malachy Doyle has made some subtle adaptations to the legend. For example, in stark contrast to the traditional portrayal of a cold, wilful and heartless fairy queen, Doyle reawakens her dormant maternal instincts when she is confronted by the pitiful condition of her son. Jac Jones's pictures evocatively enhance the text, wonderfully illuminating the interface between human and fairy worlds.

Lake of Shadows

Malachy Doyle
illustrated by Jac Jones

Pont (2002) PB £4.95
ISBN: 1 84323 076 3

This is a picture book with hidden depths. The story is a well-known Welsh legend about a beautiful lady who emerges from a lake, Llyn y Fan Fach, to win the heart of Rhys the farmer. She agrees to become his wife on the one condition that, if he strikes her three times, she will leave him at once and forever. Rhys readily accepts the condition, and they marry. Their farm prospers, and they are happy – though the lady still dreams sometimes of the freedom of deep waters. But over the years, Rhys does, quite accidentally, hit her once … twice … and then a third time. The lady, despite all that they have shared, keeps her promise and returns to the lake. This is a rather bleak story – but Malachy Doyle's retelling has great charm and humour, and also prompts deeper thoughts about the nature of the relationships between men and women. Jac Jones's illustrations strike just the right note, bringing out the humour and pathos of the story's twists and turns.

The Orchard Book of the Legends of King Arthur

Andrew Matthews
illustrated by Peter Utton

Orchard (2004) PB £8.99
ISBN: 1 84362 593 8

One of Britain's most enduring legends (witness the recent success of Kevin Crossley-Holland's *Arthur* trilogy) is given a fresh adaptation by Andrew Matthews, retold in a modern style for today's young audience. Most of the famous Arthurian tales are here, from the boy's upbringing in the household of Sir Ector, to the Sword in the Stone and the discovery of Excalibur, and from Guinevere and Lancelot to the evil Morganna and the treacherous Mordred. By updating the way the characters speak ("Of course," Arthur murmured. "Anything you say, Merlin …"; "Because I was sick of it!" said Lancelot), Andrew Matthews has made the stories accessible to younger readers, while still retaining the thrilling excitement of the legends. Peter Utton's watercolours are atmospheric, particularly in their depiction of the more mystical elements of the stories.

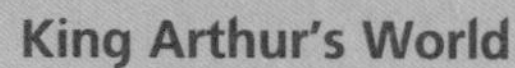

King Arthur's World

Kevin Crossley-Holland
illustrated by Hemesh Alles

Orion (2004) HB £6.99
ISBN 1 84255 101 9

This little book introduces the key figures of Arthurian legend and gives a charmingly pick 'n' mix insight into the medieval world. It is packed with lively anecdotes and entertaining lists of magical people and places. The very short chapters touch on the subjects of Heraldry, Camelot and Castle Life, Quests, Sir Kay, Magic, the Corpus Christi Carol and many others. *King Arthur's World* was originally published in 1998 with the title *The King Who Was and Will Be*, but it has been reissued as a fitting accompaniment to Crossley-Holland's *Arthur* trilogy.

The Lion Book of Tales and Legends

Lois Rock
illustrated by Christina Balit

Lion (2003) HB £12.99
ISBN: 0 7459 4239 3

Lois Rock has chosen an interesting and varied selection of stories for this book. Some of them are overtly Christian in subject matter (legends and tales from the lives of the saints) and others are more traditional folk tales in which the characters display qualities of forbearance and patience to overcome all manner of trials. Christina Balit's remarkable illustrations bring the stories to life with a bold and vibrant use of colour: the scowling merchant's daughter, the sinuous life-giving river, and the old fisherman pining for the sea are all imbued with life and emotion, as are the borders at the foot of the pages.

The Fiery Phoenix and the Lemon Princess

Margaret Mayo
illustrated by Peter Bailey

Orchard (2004) PB £3.99
ISBN: 1 84362 088 X

Before the astronomical discoveries of the last four centuries, people made up stories in order to explain how the sun worked. *The Fiery Phoenix* is one of these stories, an ancient Egyptian tale about a Bird of Fire, the symbol of the sun. *The Lemon Princess*, the other tale in the book, is an ancient Persian story about a young prince who finds a beautiful princess in a lemon tree. This is a poignant and sentimental love story that shows how good triumphs over evil. (The other titles in the *Magical Tales from Around the World* series are *The Daring Dragon*; *The Giant Sea Serpent*; *The Incredible Thunderbird*; *The Magical Mermaid*; *The Man-Eating Minotaur*; *Pegasus and the Prince* and *Unanana and the Enormous Elephant*.)

The Lady of Ten Thousand Names: Goddess Stories from Many Cultures

Burleigh Mutén
illustrated by Helen Cann

Barefoot (2002) HB £14.99
ISBN: 1 84148 047 9

This is a beautiful collection of eight stories about goddesses from around the world retold by Burleigh Mutén. Meet the Egyptian goddess Isis in *The Lady of Ten Thousand Names*, about sibling rivalry and loyalty; and the Chinese goddess Kuan Yin, worshipped for centuries as the goddess of kindness, mercy and grace, in *The Princess Who Became a Goddess*, the story of an exceptional child who finds the courage to defy her parents' wishes. *We Are All One Family* is a tale from the Lakota Sioux of North America about 'The White Buffalo Woman' who acts as a messenger for the 'Great Spirit', and *The Blessing Necklace* recounts the story of Freya, the Scandinavian goddess of love, desire, sorcery, magic and war and death, who is prepared to create a war on earth in order to get what she wants. In *Ama-Terasu's Mirror*, about the Shinto goddess of the sun from Japan – considered to be the Ancestral Mother of the Japanese people – Ama-Terasu takes drastic action to escape her brother's jealousy. Each goddess is a model of female leadership, authority and wisdom and their stories are brought to life in this poetic retelling by Burleigh Mutén and expressively portrayed in Helen Cann's rich watercolour and collage illustrations.

Did you know?

Sleeping Beauty ***was first produced as a pantomime in 1806 at Drury Lane. J. R. Planché produced an extravagant version at Convent Garden in 1840.***

Unicorns! Unicorns!

Geraldine McCaughrean
illustrated by
Sophie Windham

Orchard (1999) PB £5.99
ISBN: 1 86039 992 4

The unicorns are creatures that, like dragons and mermaids, have been imbued with myths over centuries. This interpretation of how they died out by Geraldine McCaughrean is rooted in stories from the Old Testament. When Noah called for the animals to come aboard the ark the unicorns were altruistically busy helping other lesser able animals to reach the final destination, with no concern for their own safety. This is a stunning retelling by Geraldine McCaughrean, which perfectly captures its poignancy and is matched by the glorious illustrations of Sophie Windham.

Ishtar and Tammuz: A Babylonian Myth of the Seasons

Christopher Moore
illustrated by Christina Balit

Frances Lincoln (1997) PB £4.99
ISBN: 0 7112 1099 3

This Babylonian myth has its origins some 5,000 years before the birth of Christ. Ishtar, queen of the stars, sends her son, Tammuz, to live on earth. Wherever he goes, animals follow him, everything grows in abundance and he becomes known as the 'Green One'. However, when Ishtar sees how much her son is loved she is consumed by jealousy and gives the order for him to be killed. As the earth slowly begins to die, Ishtar's people implore her to restore their 'Green One', but in order to do so, she must first battle with her sister, Allatu, who is half-woman, half-lioness and goddess of the underworld. Poetically retold, this ancient myth is brought to life by the stunning, vibrant, colourful watercolour, oil and gouache illustrations of Christina Balit, which leap off the page. There is a useful author's note at the back of the book that explains the origins of this powerful myth.

The Barefoot Book of Knights

John Matthews
illustrated by
Giovanni Manna

Barefoot (2002) HB £14.99
ISBN: 1 84148 063 0

Young Tom of Warwick is homesick when he is sent away to the castle to learn about knighthood. Under the tutelage of storyteller Master William, the young pages and squires learn about 'chivalry', the code of behaviour by which all knights try to live. Tom is enthralled by Master William's tales of the court of King Arthur, the distant realm of Prince Vladimir of Kiev, and faraway Persia and Japan. John Matthews, author of numerous books about Arthurian legends and Celtic mythology, brings together a selection of tales that will be new to many young readers. Giovanni Manna's humorous china ink and watercolour illustrations capture the atmosphere of the medieval world.

Myths & Legends

Pandora's Box

Henriette Barkow
illustrated by Diana Mayo

Mantra (2002) PB £7.50
ISBN: 1 85269 954 3

Pandora, created by Zeus, king of the gods, is given beauty from Aphrodite, wisdom from Athena, a clever tongue from Hermes and the gift of music from Apollo. Armed with these gifts, she is sent to earth, where the Titan Epimetheus falls in love with her. On their wedding day, Zeus gives them a box, which he insists must not be opened, but Pandora's curiosity gets the better of her and she cannot resist the box's allure! Once opened, however, it unleashes all manner of suffering into the world. Clearly retold by Henriette Barkow, with vivid, colourful illustrations by Diana Mayo, this is an ideal book to introduce young readers to the world of Greek mythology. This dual language edition is in both Panjabi and English and available in 21 different languages.

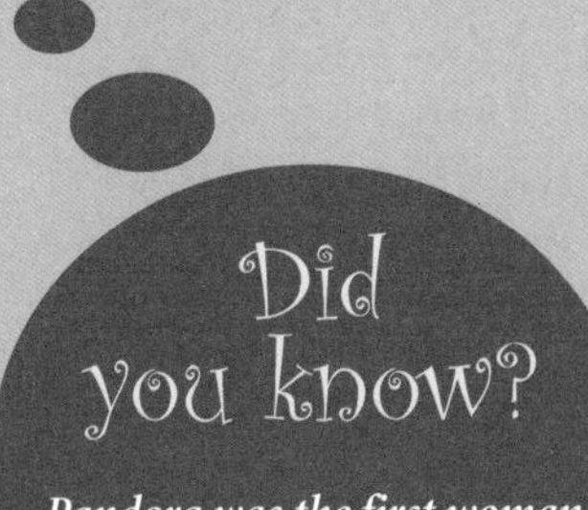

Pandora was the first woman in Greek Mythology. In 1508 the Dutch author Erasmus used the image of Pandora's box instead of the more traditional jar.

The Orchard Book of Greek Myths

Geraldine McCaughrean
illustrated by
Emma Chichester Clark

Orchard (1992) HB £12.99
ISBN: 1 85213 373 2

The Orchard Book of Greek Gods and Goddesses

Geraldine McCaughrean
illustrated by
Emma Chichester Clark

Orchard (1997) HB £12.99
ISBN: 1 86039 109 5

The Orchard Book of Greek Myths has been in print for over ten years now, and has proved itself to be a perennial bestseller. It is not hard to see why: the timeless appeal of the stories of Daedalus and Icarus, Pandora's Box, Jason and the Golden Fleece, the Wooden Horse of Troy, and King Midas retold by the award-winning author Geraldine McCaughrean and illustrated with verve by Emma Chichester Clark. The sequel, a collection of stories about Greek gods and goddesses, uses the same winning formula. Many of the myths included here are less frequently told, but Geraldine McCaughrean's lively and clear way of writing makes the unusual names and stories exciting. What is marvellous about these Greek myths is that the gods and goddesses fall prey to the same foibles as mere mortals (jealousy, love, anger, hatred), and that their reactions have devastating consequences for all concerned. Emma Chichester Clark's illustrations are less dramatic and imposing than, say, Christina Balit's, but display her trademark style; in

Gods and Goddesses, she has additionally chosen to decorate some pages with traditional Greek motifs (mosaics, statuary, pottery). These handsome volumes reveal the interlinked nature of the classical myths and their potency to both the ancient and the modern worlds.

The Orchard Book of Roman Myths

Geraldine McCaughrean
illustrated by
Emma Chichester Clark

Orchard (2003) PB £8.99
ISBN: 1 84362 308 0

This is another volume in Orchard Books's series of myths retold by Geraldine McCaughrean and illustrated by Emma Chichester Clark. There are 15 stories to choose from, some of them well-known like *Romulus and Remus*, twin boys who founded Rome, and *Chains of Love*, the story of how Venus, goddess of love married Vulcan. *Stolen Wives* is about the theft of the Sabine women: The Sabines were the most ancient and powerful Italian tribe to be absorbed into the Roman Empire. Noticing a distinct lack of women within their new city of Rome, the Romans invited the Sabines to visit them and join in the celebrations. Once the visitors had sat down to dine, the women were unceremoniously kidnapped by the Romans. All the tales included in this book will fascinate young readers. There is a brief notes section about the stories at the end of the book and a complete list of Gods and Goddesses of Rome for quick reference.

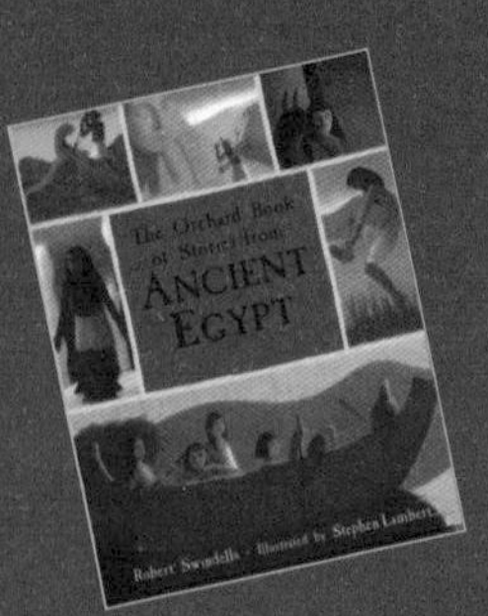

The Orchard Book of Stories from Ancient Egypt

Robert Swindells
illustrated by
Stephen Lambert

Orchard (2003) PB £8.99
ISBN: 1 84362 306 4

This well-written book about the myths and legends of ancient Egypt is a good introduction to the subject of Egyptian myths. It has the added benefit of being told in chronological order, and as a result there is more continuity between chapters than in some collections of stories. Robert Swindells starts at the beginning, relating the creation myth of Khepera, Ra, Nut and Geb, then moves on to Nut and Geb's children Isis, Osiris, Nephthys and Seth, and the tale of Seth's jealous betrayal and murder of his brother. Other famous gods such as Thoth, Hathor and Horus also make appearances; if the reader gets confused, there is a glossary to help. Stephen Lambert's pastel drawings cleverly use the colours of the desert to conjure up a feel for the ancient land and its people.

The Twelve Labours of Hercules

James Riordan
illustrated by Christina Balit

Frances Lincoln (2000) PB £6.99
ISBN: 0 7112 1391 7

Jason and the Golden Fleece

James Riordan
illustrated by Jason Cockcroft

Frances Lincoln (2003) HB £14.99
ISBN: 0 7112 2081 6

Myths & Legends

The twelve tasks of Hercules and the voyage of Jason and the Argonauts are perfect subjects for the storyteller, and have survived many retellings. In these books (which are linked in that Hercules took a break from completing his labours to join Jason's quest for the Golden Fleece) James Riordan pares the legends down without losing the essential nature of the Greek myths, namely that the lives of men and women were at the mercy of the whims of the gods (and lethal monsters), and that only courage, strength and cunning would see them to victory. Christina Balit's illustrations for *The Twelve Labours of Hercules* are extraordinary – composed from a watercolour, oil and gouache palette of browns, blues and oranges – and convey the superhuman strength of Hercules and the deadly power of his opponents. Jason Cockcroft's artwork for *Jason and the Golden Fleece* could not be more different, combining realistic illustrations and images in the black-and-red style of Greek pottery.

Sir Gawain & the Green Knight

Michael Morpurgo
illustrated by
Michael Foreman

Walker (2004) HB £14.99
ISBN: 0 7445 8646 1

Michael Morpurgo writes, 'My story is Gawain. Of all the tales of the knights of the round table, his is the most magical and one I most love to tell.' This well-known story of enchantment, chivalry and courage is compellingly retold. As the court of King Arthur sits down to enjoy the Christmas festivities, an uninvited guest – the feared Green Knight – bursts into the great hall and lays down a challenge. Sir Gawain accepts, defeats the Green Knight, but has to agree to meet him again in one year and a day. The distinctive watercolour illustrations by Michael Foreman are stunningly reproduced – especially the magnificent double-page spreads of the fiery red dragon and the headless Green Knight – and complement the narrative perfectly.

Atticus the Storyteller's 100 Greek Myths

Lucy Coats
illustrated by Anthony Lewis

Dolphin (2003) PB £9.99
ISBN: 1 84255 279 1

Atticus the sandalmaker decides to fulfil a lifetime's ambition to attend the great storytelling festival of the gods at Troy; he packs up his donkey Melissa and waves a fond farewell to his large family. On his long journey, he entertains Melissa with one hundred Greek myths, some of them very well known (Daedalus and Icarus; Medusa; Theseus and the Minotaur; King Midas), others less so (Endymion; Artemis and Actaeon; Echidna and Typhon). This big book cleverly links the narrative of Atticus's travels to the timeless myths as his experiences remind him of particular stories. The illustrations, colourful for the myths, sepia for Atticus's journey, are charmingly reminiscent of Peter Bailey's work. It won't be giving too much away to say that our storyteller eventually makes it to the competition, but does he win? The answer is revealed on the very last page.

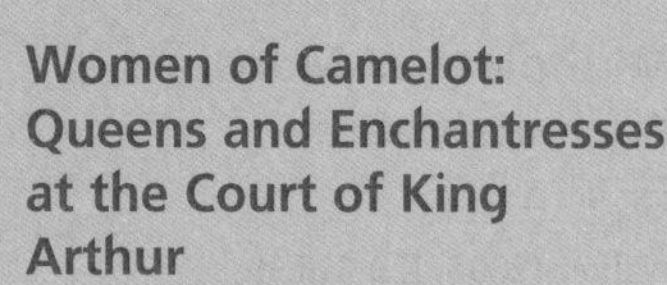

Women of Camelot: Queens and Enchantresses at the Court of King Arthur

Mary Hoffman
illustrated by Christina Balit

Frances Lincoln (2002) PB £6.99
ISBN: 0 7112 2048 4

Mary Hoffman's dramatic retellings of nine stories based on Sir Thomas Malory's *Le Morte d'Arthur* are viewed from the perspective of seven very different women, from influential queens and powerful sorceresses to ordinary women, all of whom proved to be determined and resourceful. Despite the restrictions placed upon their lives, these women often lie at the heart of the Camelot story, using love, hate, intrigue and enchantment to determine its outcome. One by one they act as narrator to tell their own story: Igrayne, the mother of King Arthur; Guinevere, Arthur's Queen; Morgan Le Fay, half-sister to Arthur and his arch enemy; and Nimu, who recounts the undoing of Merlin. Mary Hoffman – author of over 70 books for children – is a powerful storyteller; she brings a fresh perspective to the legend of Camelot. Christina Balit's illustrations are, as ever, stunning and dramatic. There is a useful section at the back of the book that lists characters and talks about sources.

Spellmakers

Julie Rainsbury
illustrated by Graham Howells

Pont (2001) PB £4.50
ISBN: 1 85902 631 1

This is a collection of magical stories to be read slowly and savoured. Julie Rainsbury has chosen seven fascinating and varied traditional stories from Wales and presented them with a magical flourish of her own. There is something interesting to think about in every story, and the atmospheric use of language makes them particularly vivid and fresh. One of the most beautiful tales in this book is about the wizard Aby Biddle and the bees, which in its quiet way suggests the devastating effects that magic can have when it is unleashed into real life! It is so good to see some less familiar traditional stories in print in a form that even reluctant folk-tale readers will enjoy. Graham Howells's illustrations bring out the humour and mystery in every story in a very appealing way.

Helping Hercules

Francesca Simon
illustrated by Tony Ross

Dolphin (2004) PB £4.99
ISBN: 1 84255 153 1

Horrid Henry author Francesca Simon has taken seven Greek myths and given them a twist by introducing an extra character in the shape of a small, and somewhat stroppy, girl named Susan. When she is sent to her room for refusing to clean out the cat's litter tray, Susan begins to play with her collection of ancient coins, including one from ancient Greece, which has magical properties. Soon she is helping Hercules with a rather larger chore than kitty litter: cleaning out the Augean stables. The book takes a fresh look at each of the myths, including Orpheus in the Underworld and King Midas, through which not only Susan, but also the reader, learns a little classical history, as well as something about family life.

The Names Upon the Harp

Marie Heaney
illustrated by P.J. Lynch

Faber and Faber (2000) HB £14.99
ISBN: 0 571 19363 3

Irish Myths & Legends

Ita Daly
illustrated by Bee Willey

Oxford University Press (2001)
HB £12.99 ISBN: 0 19 274534 4

These collections are divided according to the traditional Irish storytelling cycles – Mythological; Cuchulainn (or Ulster); and Fianna (Fenian, or Finn) – but the way in which the stories are retold and illustrated vary markedly. P.J. Lynch's wonderful watercolours in *The Names Upon the Harp* represent with passion the beautiful maidens and heroes of these tales, as well as the horrible villains and beasts. Bee Willey's illustrations are, by contrast, more gentle and humorous. Marie Heaney and Ita Daly have chosen tales that have entertained and intrigued listeners and readers for generations; while Ita Daly's modern renditions of these tales will be more accessible to readers coming to them for the first time, Marie Heaney's poetic adaptation has a more classical feel. If the stories and characters are unfamiliar to non-Gaelic readers, their themes will certainly resonate: graceful princesses in distress; ferocious giants; good against evil; fights to the death; magic and sorcery. Both authors provide a short introduction to the Cycles (Marie Heaney writes in more detail), and a useful – nay, vital – glossary of names and pronunciations.

Mythological Monsters of Ancient Greece

Sara Fanelli

Walker (2002) HB £10.99
ISBN: 0 7445 8898 7

There will never be any question of mistaking the work of Sara Fanelli for that of any other artist: the cut-out eyes, graph-paper backgrounds, crazy collages, and hand-drawn lettering all combine to make her books utterly original and unusual. This title is a collection of double-page spreads about 14 of the most gruesome monsters from the Greek myths, somehow rendered all the more shocking and bizarre in Sara Fanelli's deranged compositions. Around the illustrations she has scattered snippets of additional information about the monsters and the heroes who vanquished them. This is original work of striking quality and will stand out in any collection of books about myths and legends.

Traditional Tales from India

Vic Parker
illustrated by Nilesh Mistry

Belitha Press (2001) HB £10.99
ISBN: 1 84138 069 5

Traditional Tales from The Caribbean

Vic Parker
illustrated by
Christopher Corr

Belitha Press (2001) HB £10.99
ISBN: 1 84138 068 7

Traditional Tales from Ancient Egypt

Vic Parker

illustrated by Danuta Mayer

Belitha Press (2000) HB £10.99
ISBN: 1 84138 125 X

Traditional Tales from North America

Vic Parker

illustrated by Olivia Rayner

Belitha Press (2001) HB £10.99
ISBN: 1 84138 175 6

This series of robust hardbacks provides a brief introduction to some of the world's favourite myths and legends, from the amusing, twinkle-in-the-eye, Caribbean stories of Anansi the Spider-man, to the terrible Egyptian tales of murder and revenge; and from the dramatic attempts of the great Indian god Vishnu to overcome the wickedness of the world, to a whole range of stories from the melting-pot of North America, many of which are concerned with Nature. The illustrations for each volume are in keeping with their subject: Christopher Corr's Caribbean paintings are exuberantly bright while Olivia Rayner's North American drawings are rooted in landscape, and Danuta Mayer and Nilesh Mistry have used recognisably formal elements of Egyptian and Indian illustration respectively.

Moroccan Myths and Legends

Philippe Fix

Ragged Bears (2003) HB £19.99
ISBN: 1 85714 280 2

In this collection of traditional Moroccan myths and legends the reader is invited to take a trip through the wonderful and fantastic world of North Africa – where they will be enchanted by mythical and fantastic old stories that have been passed down from generation to generation. There are frightening tales, such as *The Girl and the Ogress*, about an orphan girl who walks through the forest and encounters a kindly-looking woman who later turns out to be a scary, hungry ogress. There are other stories that reflect the wisdom of ancient civilisation such as *The Story of Old Âref ou Aqel*, about a man who was over one hundred years old and 'knew pretty well everything'; or the dramatic tale of a selfish father who abandons his son *(The Language of the Birds)*. There are 20 tales in total and a short glossary of terms at the back of the book. Philippe Fix has vividly illustrated this volume in colour throughout, which helps create the perfect atmospheric and tone for these short stories.

Island of the Minotaur: Greek Myths of Ancient Crete

Sheldon Oberman
illustrated by Blair Drawson

Tradewind Books (2003) HB £12.95
ISBN: 1 896580 64 5

The island of Crete in the Mediterranean was home to the great but mysterious people known as the Minoans, whose mythical tales are full of heroic quests, clever tricks, and puzzles and disguises. Meet Theseus and Ariadne, Jason and Medea, Daedalus and Icarus, King Minos and Hercules, and the gods Rhea, Cronos, Zeus and Poseidon. Walk with the strange creatures of a distant world – the Ash Tree Spirits, Pan the goat boy, Talus the Bronze Giant, the Great White Bull and the monstrous Minotaur.

Beowulf

Henriette Barkow
illustrated by Alan Down

Mantra (2004) PB £7.50
ISBN: 1 84444 030 3

Beowulf: Dragonslayer

Rosemary Sutcliff

Red Fox (2001) PB £4.99
ISBN: 0 09 941713 8

Beowulf

Robert Nye

Dolphin (2004) PB £4.99
ISBN: 1 85881 076 0

Beowulf

Kevin Crossley-Holland
illustrated by Charles Keeping

Oxford University Press (2004) PB £4.99 **ISBN: 0 19 272369 3**

One of the oldest surviving poems in Old English, the story of Beowulf's titanic and bloody clash with the evil Grendel has thrilled and terrified generations of listeners and readers. Testament to its enduring popularity is the number of adaptations still available in English, of which these four give a good idea of the different ways an epic can be retold in prose. Just as the poem was adapted hundreds of years ago by oral storytellers, so each author has moulded the text, omitting some sections, changing others (Queen Wealhtheow's hair, for example, is golden, grey, or dark, depending on which version you read). Rosemary Sutcliff and Robert Nye's versions are text-based, the latter much more 'modern-sounding' than the former, which is interesting given that they were both originally published in the 1960s. Rosemary Sutcliff's writing, with its air of historical gravity and mysterious significance, is perfectly suited to the retelling of *Beowulf*.

Of the two picture books, Kevin Crossley-Holland manages the same trick as Rosemary Sutcliff, imbuing his poetic text with dark portent; Charles Keeping's utterly terrifying black ink illustrations lend an extra dimension to the writing. Henriette Barkow's adaptation is a more bland affair, and the coloured airbrush-style illustrations harbour none of the intensity of Charles Keeping's, but it is available in 18 dual language editions. Once *Beowulf* has caught the imagination of young readers – as these adaptations will ensure – it will never be forgotten.

Tales from the Old World

Kevin Crossley-Holland

Dolphin (2004) PB £4.99
ISBN: 1 85881 794 3

Award-winning author Kevin Crossley-Holland has selected a wonderful range of folk tales from across Europe. Although he includes the well-known story of *The Pied Piper of Hamelin* and a retelling of Hans Christian Andersen's *The Ugly Duckling*, he has also chosen many lesser-known tales to enthral the reader. *Godfather Death* is a Czech story about a poor man who attempts to trick 'Death' after he has made a bargain with him. *The Lady of Stavoren*, from the Netherlands, is a tale of avarice and selfishness. In addition, a Greek myth, *Persephone Rising*, and an Arthurian tale are also included, and a useful section at the back of the book contains notes about the stories and explanations of their origins.

Did you know?

'Europe' comes from the Greek word Europa. Europa was the brave daughter of King Tyre who married Zeus. In order to attract her attention, Zeus disguised himself as a bull.

Arthur High King of Britain

Michael Morpurgo
illustrated by
Michael Foreman

Egmont (2002) PB £4.99
ISBN: 0 7497 4851 6

First written by Children's Laureate Michael Morpurgo in 1994, this book was reissued in 1997 with accompanying illustrations by Michael Foreman. A young boy, in his attempt to walk around the Scilly Isles, finds himself cut off from the mainland as the sea sweeps in and the fog descends. As he loses his strength to fight the waves he slowly sinks down into the sea. Finding himself in a strange bed, unsure if he is alive or dead, the boy sees an old man sitting by the fire with his dog. He introduces himself as Arthur Pendragon and begins to recount the incredible story of Camelot. Narrated by King Arthur himself, the book captures the essence of the Camelot story – a time of chivalry and romance, evil, magic and betrayal. The black and white illustrations complement the flowing text perfectly and provide a mystical and ethereal quality. Michael Morpurgo and Michael Foreman have collaborated on a sequel to Arthur, called *The Sleeping Sword* (Egmont, 2003).

Myths & Legends

11+

In Search of a Homeland: The Story of the Aeneid

Penelope Lively
illustrated by Ian Andrew

Frances Lincoln (2001) HB £14.99
ISBN 0 7112 1728 9

The Wanderings of Odysseus: The Story of the Odyssey

Rosemary Sutcliff
illustrated by Alan Lee

Frances Lincoln (2001) PB £8.99
ISBN 0 7112 1846 3

Black Ships Before Troy: The Story of the Iliad

Rosemary Sutcliff
illustrated by Alan Lee

Frances Lincoln (2001) PB £8.99
ISBN 0 7112 1522 7

As the city of Troy burns, brave Aeneas, son of the goddess Venus, escapes with his son and father, but without his wife Creusa, who has been killed. It is his destiny to find his people a new homeland, but the struggle against enemies both mortal and immortal is a titanic one involving much hardship and many temptations along the way. Penelope Lively brings Virgil's epic vividly to life in this tremendously exciting story of gods and men. Ian Andrew's coloured-pencil drawings are simply stunning in the way they convey movement; the battle scenes in particular are mesmerising. *In Search of a Homeland* has been produced to the same high standards as Rosemary Sutcliff's books about The Iliad *(Black Ships Before Troy)* and The Odyssey *(The Wanderings of Odysseus)*; together, they form a marvellous trilogy of stories from the classical world.

Golden Myths and Legends of the World

Geraldine McCaughrean

Dolphin (1999) PB £5.99
ISBN: 1 85881 675 0

Silver Myths and Legends of the World

Geraldine McCaughrean

Dolphin (1999) PB £5.99
ISBN: 1 85881 676 9

These two volumes gather together one hundred myths and legends from around the world. *Golden Myths and Legends* contains, for example, a Chinese legend, *The Ragged Emperor* (a moral tale of virtue rewarded); a tale from Ethiopia, *Skinned Out* (about God entrusting animal messengers with crucial information); and a myth from Australia, *Rainbow Snake* (about how parts of the Australian landscape were created). In the companion volume, a Maori tale, *Dream Journey* (about the dangers, frustrations and responsibilities of leadership) is accompanied by a myth about an Egyptian goddess. Geraldine McCaughrean deftly captures the magic of these wonderful tales, many of which have been passed down from generation to generation by word of mouth.

Mythology of the World

Neil Philip
illustrated by Nicki Palin

Kingfisher (2004) HB £18.99
ISBN: 0 7534 0964 X

From the ancient Greeks to the Aztecs, people across the world have created a rich tapestry of stories, characters and beliefs to explain the mysteries of creation, and the forces of nature and death. Neil Philip examines ancient and contemporary cultures, and explores their unique myths and legends. There are a few short retellings of some of the myths, which are accompanied by colourful photographs and detailed illustrations. At the end of this excellent non-fiction book there is a checklist of other mythical figures, a glossary and an index. The author is a writer and folklorist with a particular interest in mythology and storytelling and has written widely on this subject.

100 World Myths & Legends

Geraldine McCaughrean
illustrated by Bee Willey

Orion (2001) PB £12.99
ISBN: 1 84255 035 7

The stories in this book, originally published in four separate volumes, have been collected from countries as diverse as China, Ethiopia, Polynesia, Sri Lanka, France, India, Finland, Japan, Wales, Greece, Rwanda, Ghana and many others. As Geraldine McCaughrean demonstrates, the best myths and legends deal with the complexities of human relationships, as well as the potent power of magic, courage and heroism. Her adaptations have preserved the original appeal and flavour of the stories, some of which have been in existence for hundreds of years.

Troy

Adèle Geras

Scholastic (2001) PB £5.99
ISBN: 0 439 99220 6

Set against the backdop of the Trojan war, *Troy* is essentially a love story. Due to the mischevious meddling of Aphrodite (the goddess of love), sisters Xanthe (nursemaid to the son of Hector and Andromache) and Marpessa (attendant to the beautiful Helen of Troy) both fall for the same handsome soldier, Alastor, which causes immense heartache and conflict. This epic tale tackles themes of love, friendship, war and death, and does not shy away from portraying violence and sexual experimentation. By telling her tale from the perspectives of a variety of humble characters, Adèle Geras has succeeded in making this story accessible to a contemporary audience aged 14 and over.

Viking! Myths of Gods & Monsters

Kevin Crossley-Holland

Dolphin (2002) PB £4.99
ISBN: 1-84255-283 X

The Vikings were a bloodthirsty lot, so it is no surprise to find that their myths are as well. The names may be hard to grasp, but for anyone who likes tales of blood and thunder, trickery and passion, these 17 stories will fit the bill perfectly. Among the sagas of gods, men, dwarves, monsters and giants, the legend of Loki embodies the dramatic Viking story. Loki routinely betrays men, but he goes too far when he opposes his fellow gods by refusing to let wise Balder leave Niflheim, the place of the dead. Loki, as punishment, is trussed up in his son's guts in a cave, where a poisonous snake drips venom into his face… Kevin Crossley-Holland is a great teller of stories; his love of the English language is marvellously suited to the task of retelling these gory tales.

Arthur: The Seeing Stone

Kevin Crossley-Holland

Orion (2001) PB £5.99
ISBN: 0 75284 429 6

Set on the border between England and Wales in AD 1199, this is the story of Arthur de Caldicot, a 13-year-old boy who is anxious to become a knight. His putative father's friend Merlin gives him a 'seeing stone', in which he sees events from the early life of Arthur Pendragon; these seem to reflect or anticipate events in his own life. Kevin Crossley-Holland's fascinating story, rich in historical detail and the mysteries of the Arthurian legend, brings to life the grubby reality of feudal life in the Middle Ages.

Arthur: At the Crossing Places

Kevin Crossley-Holland

Orion (2002) PB £5.99
ISBN: 1 84255 200 7

The second instalment in the *Arthur* trilogy is set in AD 1200. Arthur, now aged 14, leaves Caldicot and his childhood behind to take up a position as squire to Lord Stephen. Finding his feet in a new environment, he has to negotiate several awkward situations at the manor while making preparations to accompany Lord Stephen on Crusade. He also continues to follow the adventures of King Arthur and his Knights in his 'seeing stone'. Written in bite-sized chapters, the sharpness of the writing is as effective as ever, setting the stage for a gripping conclusion to the trilogy.

Arthur: King of the Middle March

Kevin Crossley-Holland

Orion (2004) PB £5.99
ISBN: 1 84255 155 8

The final volume of the *Arthur* trilogy opens in Venice, where Arthur has joined Lord Stephen on the Fourth Crusade. Men are beginning to turn against one another, causing the young knight to question the true meaning of the holy war. Arthur continues to find in his 'seeing stone' many parallels between his life and the adventures of King Arthur and his Knights. Kevin Crossley-Holland is a poet with a true feeling for words. The sights and smells of the journey are beautifully realised and the reader identifies with Arthur's excitement and horror, as well as his desperate desire to know his mother, his uncertainty about his future and above all his determination to be a good knight. The author raises many issues that are relevant to us today and weaves them skilfully into a novel that is packed with historical detail and thrilling adventure.

Myths & Legends

Anthony Horowitz
illustrated by Francis Mosley

Kingfisher (2004) PB £ 5.99
ISBN: 0 7534 1017 6

Anthony Horowitz is a best-selling children's author, best known for his fiction, particularly the highly acclaimed and pacy *Point Blanc.* Now he has brought his storytelling skills to bear on this selection of myths and legends, which includes ancient tales from Egypt *(Isis and Osiris)*, Greece *(The Achilles Heel; Pandora's Box)*, Rome *(Romulus and Remus)* and many other countries. The book is illustrated with black-and-white drawings, and contains an index of names featured in the stories.

Corbenic

Catherine Fisher

Red Fox (2002) PB £5.99
ISBN: 0 09 943848 8

Desperate to escape his alcoholic mother, Cal sets off one bleak, rainy night to join his uncle in Chepstow, in order to start a new life. On the way, he falls asleep on the train, awakes in a panic and alights at the wrong station, to find himself caught in another world: Corbenic. Resonant with Arthurian echoes (much of the action takes place at the castle of the Fisher King), this is an ambitious and powerfully-written tale, which links one young man's painful quest for self-knowledge with that of the ancient legend of the Holy Grail.

The Snow-Walker Trilogy

Catherine Fisher

Red Fox (2003) PB £5.99
ISBN: 0 09 944806 8

This single volume contains all three of Catherine Fisher's Snow-Walker books *(The Snow-Walker's Son, The Empty Hand* and *The Soul Thieves).* This spellbinding modern version of a Norse saga is about Kari – who has been abandoned and banished by his evil sorceress mother, but rescued by the loyalty of others – and Jessa, whose family has also suffered at the hands of the sorceress's evil magic. This is a thrilling tale of adventure, loyalty, courage and fear and of good against evil. Catherine Fisher's narrative flows effortlessly with fine descriptive imagery; a serious subtext invites the reader to examine not only the original saga tradition but also the complexity of human relationships.

The Oracle

Catherine Fisher

Hodder (2003) PB £5.99
ISBN: 0 340 84376 4

The ancient god of a desert land rules his people by the means of an Oracle, whose commands are interpreted by the High Priestess. But are they really his commands? Mirany, a new Bearer, has to carry the scorpions used in ritual ceremonies, seeks to uncover the truth, but her position puts her in real danger. Her only allies are Seth, a scribe and tomb robber, and Oblek, a mad musician. *The Oracle* is a spare and electrifying read, full of heart-stopping moments.

Troll Fell

Katherine Langrish

Collins (2004) HB £10.99
ISBN: 0 00 717071 8

Katherine Langrish's atmospheric debut novel is inspired by Viking legends of the tenth-century. Following the death of his father, Peer is forced to go and live with his hideous money-grasping uncles, Baldur and Grim Grimsson and their vicious dog, Grendel, at their mill near Troll Fell. Peer lives a life of servitude, with only the company of his faithful dog, Loki, until he meets the Nis, his uncles' house spirit, and the strong-minded Hilde. The Grimssons want riches and they will do anything to get them. Peer and Hilde must find a way to foil the evil transaction that they have made with the sinister, cunning and ruthless trolls who live under Troll Fell. This novel is intensely engaging and the bleak landscape and atmosphere are evocative. Katherine Langrish has been a storyteller for many years and her pacy style carries the reader through this story effortlessly.

Did you know?

In earlier versions of* Goldilocks and the Three Bears, *the intruder featured in the story was an old woman

Modern Versions of Traditional Fairy Tales

In this section you will find humorous modern reinventions of well-known fairy tales, as well as fictional narratives for older readers, which embellish the original tales.

Modern Versions of Traditional Fairy Tales

Under 6

Not Again, Little Red Riding Hood!

Kate Clynes
illustrated by Louise Daykin

Mantra (2003) PB £7.50
ISBN: 1 85269 963 9

This is what happened to Little Red Riding Hood when she met the wolf a second time! Little Red Riding Hood sets off into the woods to deliver cookies to her dad. Along the way she meets some very hungry characters from well-loved tales: Rapunzel with the golden hair, the Three Little Bears, the Three Billy Goats and finally her true adversary, the big, bad wolf! This is a fun book that children will enjoy and is ideal for reading aloud. The bold, colourful illustrations complement the text. A dual language version of this book is available in Bengali and English.

The Frog Princess

Jan Ormerod
illustrated by Emma Damon

Hodder (2004) PB £4.99
ISBN: 0 340 87372 8

In a clever twist to the plot of this familiar Brothers Grimm story, it is the 'frog' who has become a princess; she can only be returned to her original state by the kindness of another frog. Helen Damon's highly atmospheric and expressive pictures add an extra dimension to this tale.

Fairytale News

Colin and Jacqui Hawkins

Walker (2004) HB £10.99
ISBN: 0 7445 9257 7

Jack lives in Tangled Wood with Mother Hubbard but they have no food or money. Fortunately he manages to get a job in the local newsagents, delivering *Fairytale News* to well-known characters from the fairy tale world. The Three Bears (from *Goldilocks and the Three Bears*) are first, then Mrs and Mr Hood (from *Little Red Riding Hood*), and finally the Giant (from *Jack and the Beanstalk*). In the best tradition of fairy tales, this book starts with 'once upon a time' and finishes with 'and they lived happily ever after'. It also contains a free newspaper, which features news, horoscopes, small ads, items for sale and information galore about Fairyland's most famous characters.

The Three Little Wolves and the Big Bad Pig

Eugene Trivizas
illustrated by Helen Oxenbury

Egmont (2003) PB £5.99
ISBN: 1 4052 0945 3

This is an amusing modern version of the 'Three Little Pigs' tale. Three little wolves set out into the world to build themselves a house, but they have not bargained on the big bad pig thwarting them at every turn! Eugene Trivizas's humorous tale can scarcely fail to delight, and will have children giggling from the outset. Helen Oxenbury's illustrations are delightful and full of comic zest; it is impossible not to love the cute little wolves and the roguish big bad pig!

Modern Versions of Traditional Fairy Tales

Cinderella and the Hot Air Balloon

Ann Jungman
illustrated by Russell Ayto

Frances Lincoln (1995) PB £5.99
ISBN: 0 7112 1051 9

This funny version of *Cinderella* will really appeal to young children. Cinderella is not interested in going to the boring old ball so she throws her own party instead! When Prince Charming, who likes to be known as 'Bill', turns up, he discovers that he has some rather unexpected tastes in common with Cinderella: climbing trees, riding bareback, skating on thin ice and running barefoot! Russell Ayto's colourful, cartoon-like illustrations are full of humour and vibrancy and complement the pacy style of Ann Jungman's narrative.

The Pea and the Princess

Mini Grey

Jonathan Cape (2003) HB £10.99
ISBN: 0 224 06459 2

The Pea and the Princess, shortlisted for the CILIP Kate Greenaway Medal 2003, is the 'real' story of the princess and the pea, from pod to palace. The story is narrated by the pea, which recounts events from its own perspective! Mini Grey's amusing and enjoyable book has entertaining caricature-style illustrations that give the story a contemporary feel (a pile of mattresses in the shape of a hamburger; 'photographs' of other well-known fairy tale princesses).

Did you know?

Rapunzel is the German for 'Rampion', a type of harebell with delicate blue flowers

Once Upon a Time

Niki Daly

Frances Lincoln (2004) PB £5.99
ISBN: 0 7112 1993 1

Sairie, a South African girl who has difficulty reading, is mocked by her classmates. She makes friends with an old lady, Ou Missus, who lives across the veld and who helps her overcome her fears by suggesting they read *Cinderella* together in her broken-down Cadillac. This is a heart-warming tale of friendship that will appeal not only to reluctant readers but also to those who lack self-confidence and find it hard to make friends. The illustrations are full of movement and life and conjure up another place and culture superbly.

Modern Versions of Traditional Fairy Tales

6-8

Rapunzel: A Groovy Fairy Tale

Lynn Roberts
illustrated by David Roberts

Pavilion (2003) HB £9.99
ISBN: 1 84365 009 6

Cinderella: An Art Deco Love Story

Lynn Roberts
illustrated by David Roberts

Pavilion (2003) PB £5.99
ISBN: 1 84365 013 4

Lynn and David Roberts have given two classic fairy tales a distinctly individual and amusing twist, thereby proving their endless appeal, adaptability, and relevance to all generations and ages. Rapunzel lives on the top floor of a 1970s concrete tower block with her nasty Aunt Edna, who refuses to let her out of the flat. The lifts in the building don't work, so Edna calls up to Rapunzel to let down her long red hair. Inevitably, a handsome young man comes along … David Roberts's illustrations are packed with references to the 70s: a lava lamp, flared trousers, punks, thick-soled shoes. Rapunzel is clearly a Kate Bush fan (she has a poster of her and two of her LPs – *The Kick Inside* and *Lionheart*), but she also likes John Travolta, Abba, Stevie Wonder, Marc Bolan, Elton John, Blondie and David Bowie. *Cinderella* is similarly full of period detail: Tiffany lamps, Clarice Cliff pottery, and 1920s fashions. Great fun.

The Real Fairy Storybook: Stories the Fairies Tell Themselves

Georgie Adams
illustrated by Sally Gardner

Dolphin (1999) PB £5.99
ISBN: 1 85881 681 5

Each story in this collection of modern versions of fairy stories is beautifully introduced by the fairies themselves. One of the stories is about a seahorse who gets kidnapped by the ugly Kelpies, but is miraculously saved by ingenious good fairies; another features a spoilt little princess with bad manners whose hair starts to grow endlessly after a spell is cast upon her. Sally Gardner's quirky and detailed illustrations possess a special charm that will appeal to children and adults alike.

The Nightspinners

Kate Petty
illustrated by
Mary Claire Smith

Orion (2003) HB £9.99
ISBN: 1 85881 836 2

Ariane is a weaver who lives in a house in the woods. Her only companions are animals, insects and spiders, which weave their beautiful and elaborate gleaming threads. The wicked, heartless Queen orders Ariane to weave a silk dress that glistens like the morning dew. This must be done by dawn, or her head will be chopped off! Luckily Ariane's love and respect for spiders is rewarded when they decide to help her, but not before they teach the nasty Queen a lesson. Mary Claire Smith's paintings are evocative and delicate.

8-11

Modern Versions of Traditional Fairy Tales

Into the Forest

Anthony Browne

Walker (2004) HB £12.99
ISBN: 0 7445 9797 8

A boy is suddenly woken up in the middle of the night by a terrible sound. The next day he discovers that his father has left home and his mother doesn't seem to know when he will be coming back. She gives him a basket of food to take to his Grandma who is ill in bed. On the way, he encounters a boy with a cow, a girl with golden hair, two abandoned children and a red coat hanging from a tree trunk. The boy runs away to Grandma's cottage where he finds an unusual surprise awaiting him! Each wonderful illustration contains many references to many popular fairy tales, *Cinderella*, *Rapunzel* and *Jack and the Beanstalk* among them.

Ella's Big Chance

Shirley Hughes

The Bodley Head (2003) HB £10.99
ISBN: 0 370 37265 9

Subtitled 'a fairy tale retold', the winner of the 2003 CILIP Kate Greenaway Medal is an updated version of the Cinderella story, set in the glamorous Art Deco period of the 1920s. Ella is a talented dressmaker who slaves over her sewing machine while her vain step-mother and two step-sisters spend all their time trying on the wonderful dresses in her father's dress shop. The stunning clothes depicted in the book, with their inventive patterns and intricate details, were all designed by Shirley Hughes, who drew inspiration from the French couturiers of the period. In addition, her outstanding craftsmanship can be seen in her palette of oranges, pinks and purples, and the cameo black-and-white drawings, which extend the narrative. Her illustrations of Ella and the Prince dancing are particularly charming, reminiscent of Fred Astaire films. *Ella's Big Chance* shows one of our best children's illustrators at the height of her powers.

Cinderboy (Seriously Silly Stories)

Laurence Anholt
illustrated by Arthur Robins

Orchard (2002) PB £3.99
ISBN: 1 84121 404 3

Laurence Anholt plays fast and loose with the Cinderella story by giving it a modern-day setting and changing the sex of the central character, who, as a boy, naturally lives with his stepfather and stepbrothers. The family is mad about football, but when they go to see Royal Palace, their favourite team, play, poor Cinderboy is left behind to do all the household chores. Later, however, a 'good TV Godmother' appears on television and instructs Cinderboy to press the bottom of the remote control. As if by magic, Cinderboy is instantly transported to the football pitch and becomes a true hero. Arthur Robins's quirky illustrations are the perfect match to this hilarious tale.

Daft Jack and the Bean Stack

Laurence Anholt
illustrated by Arthur Robins

Orchard (2002) PB £3.99
ISBN: 1 84121 408 6

Daft Jack can't believe his luck when he swaps his old cow Daisy for a whole tin of baked beans, but his mother is furious. Then they realise it is a lucky tin and they have won a prize – an endless supply of baked beans! They stack the tins in a corner of their field, but what will Jack find when he climbs the bean stack? Laurence Anholt uses simple vocabulary, yet instantly manages to capture the readers' imagination with the familiarity of the tale and the daft humour. Funny line drawings complement the text perfectly. This is another great title in the series of *Seriously Silly Stories*, which are ideal for early and reluctant readers.

Ghostyshocks and the Three Scares

Laurence Anholt
illustrated by Arthur Robins

Orchard (2001) PB £3.99
ISBN: 1 84121 532 5

Ghostyshocks is terrified of everything. When she enters a deserted cottage in the forest, she is so nervous that she spills food down her dress and breaks a chair. Hiding in the smallest bed, she desperately hopes she will not be discovered. This alternative retelling of *Goldilocks and the Three Bears* has brilliant line drawings and speech bubbles that add to the hilarity.

Revolting Rhymes

Roald Dahl
illustrated by Quentin Blake

Puffin (2001) PB £6.99
ISBN: 0 14056 8247

This is a hilarious collection of some well-loved fairy tales, cleverly reinvented by Roald Dahl. When the giant 'smells an Englishman' in *Jack and the Beanstalk*, the hapless youth gets in trouble from his Mum for not washing more often. The heroine of *Little Red Riding Hood* pulls out a pistol and shoots the wolf dead before using his fur to make herself a coat! Then she skips off to rescue a poor little pig in the *The Three Little Pigs*. A not-so-vulnerable Cinderella demands to go to the 'disco' at the Palace and ends up running around at midnight in her underwear! All these terrific stories are written in verse and are gorgeously decorated by Quentin Blake's glorious illustrations.

The Seven Dwarfs

Etienne Delessert

Creative Editions (2002) HB £10.99
ISBN: 1 56846 139 9

This lovely gift book is an unusual interpretation of the tale of Snow White, narrated by one of the seven dwarfs. As well as retelling the story from his own perspective, Stephane also describes the festivities prior to Snow White's wedding to the prince; how magnificently the guests are entertained by the King; and how he and his brothers came to be Dukes of the Forest. Although stylishly set out, the pages are slightly text-laden at times due to the small font size. Nevertheless, this is a unique version of a classic tale, beautifully told and stunningly illustrated by Etienne Delessert, the creator of more than 80 children's books and winner of the Premio Grafico at the Bologna Children's Book Fair.

Modern Versions of Traditional Fairy Tales

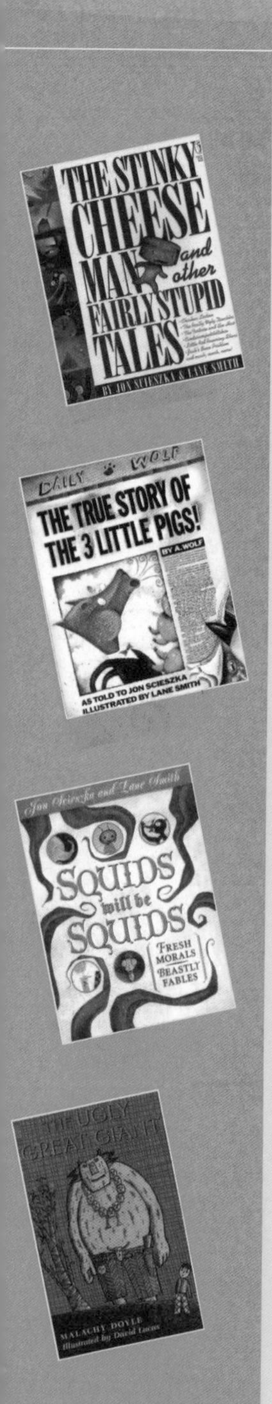

The Stinky Cheese Man and Other Fairly Stupid Tales

Jon Scieszka
illustrated by Lane Smith

Puffin (1993) PB £6.99
ISBN: 0 14 054896 3

The True Story of the Three Little Pigs

Jon Scieszka
illustrated by Lane Smith

Puffin (1991) PB £5.99
ISBN: 0 14 054056 3

Squids will be Squids: Fresh Morals, Beastly Fables

Jon Scieszka
illustrated by Lane Smith

Puffin (1999) PB £6.99
ISBN: 0 14 056523 X

Jon Scieszka and Lane Smith (and Smith's wife, Molly Leach, whose design work is integral to the success of these books) have collaborated on some of the best – and funniest - children's books of the last 20 years. Jon Scieszka's skewed and imaginative takes on some of Western culture's most loved stories are perfectly complemented by Lane Smith's wacky illustrations (which are works of art in their own right). The original tales are easily recognisable in these adaptations, but, by turning them on their head, Scieszka makes us look at them in a new way: *The Stinky Cheese Man* is an unsavoury version of the *Gingerbread Man* (not that it does him much good); the Ugly Duckling grows up to be a Really Ugly Duck; and Frog only pretends to be a prince in disguise, leaving the poor princess to wipe slime from her lips.

In similar style, *The True Story of the Three Little Pigs* lets us in on what really happened to the little porkers. *Squids Will Be Squids* is a hallucinogenic ride through the territory of Aesop's fables, but the morals of these stories – and the ways that the author and illustrator arrive at them – have to be seen to be believed: Skunk, Musk Ox and Cabbage come to understand the meaning of 'he who smelt it, dealt it'; Straw realises why he shouldn't play with Matches (it's not what you think); and Little Walrus learns that although telling the truth is important, sometimes it is best to omit some of the details. And the moral of all this? These great books bring new life to the fairy tale genre and deserve a place on every bookcase in the land!

The Ugly Great Giant

Malachy Doyle
illustrated by David Lucas

Orchard (2004) PB £3.99
ISBN: 1 84362 241 6

This new fairy tale is firmly grounded in tradition. Out walking one day, Sam is surprised by the sudden appearance of an ugly great giant, who proceeds to challenge him to a game of cards. Sam wins twice, but, in spite of a wise old woman's warnings, he plays a third time, loses and looks set to lose his head as well. With all the excitement, humour and fear we expect to find in the best fairy tales, but also incorporating elements from Greek legend, Malachy Doyle relates how Sam not only avoids his fate but also gets to marry the giant's daughter. True to tradition, there are several macabre touches, which allow readers a vicarious dose of Grimm-inspired terror. David Lucas's woodcut-style illustrations feel both reassuringly traditional and wittily modern.

Modern Versions of Traditional Fairy Tales

11+

The Goose Girl

Shannon Hale

Bloomsbury (2003) HB £12.99
ISBN: 0 7475 6419 1

This is a wonderfully rich retelling of a Brothers Grimm tale, set in medieval Germany. Following her betrothal – arranged by her mother, the Queen of Kildenree – Anidora sets out on a long journey to the city of Bayern. Betrayed by her lady-in-waiting and her supporters, Ani finds herself completely alone. She has to muster the courage to obtain an audience with the king to tell him of the treachery that has been committed. This eloquent debut novel has a complex plot, lovely imagery, and a strong female protagonist. It is an adventurous tale about the devastation of betrayal, and is full of danger, suspense and surprising twists. (Shannon Hale's new novel *Enna Burning* tells the story of Enna, Ani's friend in *The Goose Girl.*)

Beauty: A Retelling of the Story of Beauty & the Beast

Robin McKinley

Corgi (2004) PB £5.99
ISBN: 0 552 54863 4

Beauty believes that she is plain and awkward compared to her two older sisters. When their father's business collapses, they are forced to leave the city and begin a new life in the countryside. On his return from a visit to the city, Beauty's father chances upon a magical castle and accepts hospitality of an invisible owner. As he sets out to return home, he plucks a magnificent crimson rose from the garden, which results in a fearsome Beast exacting from him a terrible promise. He must forfeit his life, or one of his daughters must live with the Beast forever. Beauty accepts the challenge. Robin McKinley respectful adaptation of this famous story retains its central enchanting theme – that love can conquer all. Her prose is elegant and her characterisation thoughtful; for her, Beast is a sad and mysterious figure rather than a frightening or beastly one.

The Frog Princess

E. D. Baker

Bloomsbury (2002) PB £5.99
ISBN: 0 7475 6074 9

This delightful story is a very witty take on the original Brothers Grimm tale *The Frog Prince*. Princess Esmeralda (Emma) hates being a princess; she is not particularly beautiful, has a laugh like a braying donkey, and is extremely clumsy. In an attempt to escape the dreaded Prince Jorge, whom her mother wishes her to marry, Emma goes down to the swamp where she meets a talking frog. He tells her he is really a prince and persuades her to kiss him so that the spell he is under can be broken, but instead Esmeralda finds herself transformed ... into a frog!

Modern Versions of Traditional Fairy Tales

Spindle's End: A Tale of Magic and Adventure

Robin McKinley

Corgi (2003) PB £5.99 ISBN: 0 5525 4822 7

Spindle's End is a retelling of *The Sleeping Beauty*. When Katriona attends the princess's christening she has no idea that she will be returning to Foggy Bottom with an extra bundle! It is up to Katriona and her Aunt to keep the princess, known as Rosie, hidden from the wicked Pernicia, who placed a curse on her and will stop at nothing to destroy both her and the kingdom. As Rosie grows up, she develops a unique gift of 'beast-speak', which enables her to talk to, and be understood by, animals. With Rosie's 21st birthday fast approaching, Katriona and Aunt know that they will have to tell her who she really is and warn her about the terrible danger that awaits her.

Did you know?

Romulus and Remus, in Roman mythology, were twin brothers who founded the city of Rome. The infants were nursed by a female wolf

Hans Christian Andersen (1805- 1875)

2005 marks the bicentenary of the birth of Hans Christian Andersen. For over 150 years this remarkable writer's memorable tales have survived the test of time, treasured by readers of all ages. As more and more contemporary books are aimed by publishers at a 'crossover' market, it is worth noting that Andersen always insisted his stories were written for everyone; eventually he even dropped the words 'told for children' from the title of his tales. In his autobiography, *The Fairy Tale of My Life**, he wrote, 'I had arrived at the conviction that people of different ages were equally amused by the tales.'

Hans Christian Andersen's remarkable life story could have been the subject of one of his own tales. His rise from the slums to high society – a 'rags to riches' tale – is an abiding theme of many of his fairy stories. Andersen was born in Odense, Denmark on 2nd April 1805, the son of a shoemaker and a washerwoman. At the age of 14, he left his family to go to Copenhagen in the hope of becoming a performer; for several years he managed to get small parts at the Royal Theatre. By the age of 23, however, he had decided to be a writer. After trying his hand at many literary forms (poetry, plays, novels and travel books), his genius found its true expression in his famous fairy tales.

Andersen travelled extensively and was inspired by the folk tales that he collected throughout Europe and Asia. He was first and foremost a storyteller, and one of the first writers to adapt the storytelling techniques of the oral tradition to express thoughts and episodes from his own life.

Tales Told for Children was published in 1835, but it was not until 1846 that the first translated selection of his fairy stories appeared in English. The tales quickly established themselves as classics; they have since been published in innumerable editions, translated into more than 100 languages and illustrated in a wide variety of styles all over the world.

The appeal of these fairy tales lies in the fact that Andersen speaks directly to the reader. He wrote about the universal truths of human nature: good and evil, and happiness and sadness. His characters (the Little Mermaid; the Ugly Duckling; the Emperor of China) all learn from their experiences, and in turn provide the reader with lessons and morals about life. From Andersen we learn that beauty is more than skin deep; that nature's gifts are precious and that the sacrifices we make for love are at the heart and soul of who we are.

Andersen's enormous contribution to literature is recognised in a number of ways around the world. The *Hans Christian Andersen Award* is the most prestigious prize for children's literature; established in 1956, this biennial medal is the highest international recognition that an author and illustrator of a children's book can receive. International Children's Book Day, which aims to inspire a love of reading and draw attention to children's books, has been celebrated on the anniversary of Andersen's birth since 1967. And in June 2004, an exhibition about Andersen's life and work opened at the house in Odense where he was born.

These events, and the many editions of Andersen's work that are still available – of which only a sample has been reviewed in this publication – are testament to the great and lasting appeal of one of literature's most renowned writers.

For further information visit the Odense Tourist Information website (details available in English).
www.odenseturist.dk

The Hans Christian Andersen Foundation lists all the events being organised for the bicentenary.
www.hca2005.com

**The Fairy Tale of My Life: An Autobiography*
Hans Christian Andersen
New Edition with an introduction by Naomi Lewis
Cooper Square Press (2000) PB £17.95 ISBN: 0 8154 1105 7

Illustration from *Tales of Hans Christian Andersen* translated by Naomi Lewis
and illustrated by Joel Stewart. Illustration © 2004 Joel Stewart
Reproduced by permission of Walker Books Ltd, London SE1 5HJ

Secondary Sources

Folk and fairy tales have long been subjected to academic scrutiny from a variety of perspectives. This brief selection of secondary sources will provide those interested in reading further, with several starting points.

The Uses of Enchantment:
The Meaning and Importance of Fairy Tales
Bruno Bettelheim
Penguin (1991) PB £10.99 ISBN: 0 14 013727 0

The Oxford Companion to Children's Literature
Edited by Humphrey Carpenter and Mari Prichard
Oxford University Press (1999) PB £25.00 ISBN: 0 19 860228 6

International Companion Encyclopedia of Children's Literature
Edited by Peter Hunt
Routledge (2002) PB £19.99 ISBN: 0 415 28559 3

The English Fable:
Aesop and Literary Culture 1651-1740
Jayne Elizabeth Lewis
Cambridge University Press (1996) HB ISBN: 0 521 48111 2

Seeing Through the Mother Goose Tales:
Visual Turns in the Writings of Charles Perrault
Philip Lewis
Stanford University Press (1996) HB £36.95 ISBN: 0 8047 2410 5

The Cinderella Story:
The Origins and Variations of the Story Known as 'Cinderella'
Neil Philip
Penguin (1989) PB £6.99 ISBN: 0 14 059504 x

The Classic Fairy Tales
Iona and Peter Opie
Oxford University Press (1980) PB ISBN: 0 19 520219 8

Secondary Sources

Fairy Tales and After:
From Snow White to E. B. White
Roger Sale
Harvard University Press (1978) HB ISBN: 0 674 29157 3

Classic Fairy Tales (Norton Critical Editions)
Maria Tatar (Editor)
Norton (1998) PB £8.50 ISBN: 0 393 97277 1

From the Beast to the Blonde:
On Fairy Tales and Their Tellers
Marina Warner
Vintage (1995) PB £12.99 ISBN: 0 09 947951 6

The Cambridge Guide to Children's Books in English
Edited by Victor Watson
Cambridge University Press (2001) HB £45.00 ISBN: 0 521 55064 5

Fairy Tales and the Art of Subversion:
The Classical Genre for Children and the Process of Civilization
Jack Zipes
Routledge (1995) PB £16.99 ISBN: 0 415 90513 3

Happily Ever After:
Fairy Tales, Children and the Cultural Industry
Jack Zipes
Routledge (1997) PB £15.99 ISBN: 0 415 91851 0

The Oxford Companion to Fairy Tales
Edited by Jack Zipes
Oxford University Press (2000) HB £35.00 ISBN: 0 19 860115 8

The Trials & Tribulations of Little Red Riding Hood:
Versions of the Tale in Sociocultural Context
Jack Zipes
Routledge (1993) HB £18.99 ISBN: 0 415 90835 3

Title Index

H

I

J

K

L

R

S

T

U

V

W

Author/Illustrator Index

A

B

C

D

Notes

Notes